BEKEN OF COWES

THE NEW

Ocean Thoroughbreds

BEKEN OF COWES

THE NEW
Ocean
Thoroughbreds

TEXT BY
BOB FISHER

PHOTOGRAPHS BY
A. KEITH BEKEN AND KENNETH J. BEKEN

HARRAP
LONDON

Glossary

IOR   International Offshore Rule
IYRU   International Yacht Racing Union
RORC   Royal Ocean Racing Club
SORC   Southern Ocean Racing Conference, Florida

The specifications of the yachts in THE NEW OCEAN
THOROUGHBREDS relate to the year in which their pictures
were taken.
    Measurements of yachts registered in the United States of
America and Canada are given in the linear as well as the metric
system.

Opposite title page: Cowes Harbour
Illustration above: The Admiral's Cup

First published in Great Britain 1988
by HARRAP LIMITED
19-23 Ludgate Hill, London EC4M 7PD

© Beken of Cowes 1988

ISBN 0 245 54472-0

Designed by Michael R. Carter

Printed and bound in Hong Kong by
arrangement with Regent Publishing

CONTENTS

Forewords by BEKEN OF COWES

I am attending the Sailing Week at the port of Brest in that beautiful part of France, Brittany. The young Frenchman, Philippe Monnet, has just arrived in his trimaran *Kriter*. He looks as though he is returning from a cool day's fishing: in fact he has just sailed round the world single-handed in 123 days without stopping, breaking another record the while.

In the distance, 'high-tech' trimarans, launched only days before, are approaching fast, battling for line honours. Each resembles a huge albatross skimming low over the sea, and in seconds these giants — with a wingspan of over 60 feet — are upon us, travelling at 25 knots in only light airs and posing yet another challenge to the art of photographing at sea.

I have been taking pictures of ships and yachts for the past 50 years and over that time yacht design, it seems to me, has changed from the sublime to the ridiculous and back to the sublime. Hulls have progressed from wood to polyester, steel and aluminium and sails from Egyptian cotton through nylon to Mylar film. And although the 'elder statesmen' of yacht design are still at work, with the advent of the technological age more and more young designers have come to the fore. My son, Kenneth, and I have had the pleasure of meeting many of the yachting world's top designers and the privilege of talking to their boats' crews. Their dedication and enthusiasm, I am glad to say, has remained steadfast over the years — with perhaps one variation. The winchmen of today, I understand, are given raw meat to eat rather than beer to drink!

In this, our centenary year, *Beken of Cowes* is proud to present the very best of the world's racing yachts in *The New Ocean Thoroughbreds*. We make no apology for including one or two 'oldies' for, although they may be older than most, they are still racing the oceans, albeit in a new gown. We wish you 'bon voyage'.

A. Keith Beken FRPS

Most yachtsmen presume that the name *Beken* refers to an old sea-salt who took his first photograph in 1888 and who, by some miraculous preservation, continues to rush round today in speed-boats and helicopters. It was therefore not easy to be accepted as the 'new blood' in the lineage of *Beken of Cowes*, following as I did in the footsteps of my grandfather and father, Frank and Keith Beken.

Three full generations have now brought the name of *Beken of Cowes* through one hundred years of marine photography. To many, it would seem that *Beken* was around when sailing first started. In fact, a certain Royal prince jokingly asked recently whether we had any photographs of the Spanish Armada!

Frank Beken certainly had to be inventive to survive. It was he who rejected the old bellows type of camera as impractical, in favour of a screw-thread focus box camera fired by biting a rubber ball. He also had to cope with large schooners and J-class yachts from a wooden rowing dinghy and an 8-knot launch. How different it is today when we use the best Rollei and Hasselblad cameras from two 35-knot launches. But the style of photography has changed little. There are many more yachts at sea nowadays and often their design comes straight from a computer keyboard, but it is up to the eye behind the camera to compose a 'picture' instead of a snapshot.

I recently compared photographs taken in the summer of 1987 of the restored *Velsheda, Vagrant, Sumurun* and *Altair*, to find that they echoed closely those taken by my grandfather. The only difference seemed to be that today we have all the advantages of colour film, whereas he did not. Many people would contend, though, that his fine studies in the rich and warm sepia brown tint cannot be bettered, even by today's technicolour.

The pages in this book should stir the salt-water that runs in most yachtsmen's veins, and few could fail to be intrigued by Bob Fisher's text. For me, they bring back memories of when, where and how the book's photographs were taken. From being thrown around in a tiny helicopter above the Indian Ocean off Perth shooting twelve-metres in the America's Cup, to a near sinking in a chartered speed-boat in the Mediterranean whilst photographing the Sardinia Cup. From battling in Force Nine gales to photograph maxi-yachts in 1983, to watching sharks circle my rubber dinghy while working in the Canaries! But then, everyone who ever goes to sea has a story to tell and, fortunately for us, every picture tells its own story.

Kenneth J. Beken FRPS

Sixty Years On

Although I have been photographing yachts for only twenty years, it often seems more like a hundred. This is probably because each working day a great many *Beken* photographs pass before my eyes; some taken only yesterday, others depicting the century of sail that has been captured through the lenses of my father and grandfather.

The style of 'marine portraiture' appears to have changed little over three generations; the skills involved in photographing a boat today are not very different from those required at the turn of the century. True, the craft have changed, but the manner and resulting quality of their portrayal has not. Perhaps a look at Frank Beken's ideas from the 1920s on how to photograph a yacht will enlighten and entertain the reader.

Kenneth J. Beken FRPS

ON PHOTOGRAPHING A YACHT.

MARINE photography is an art that requires long years of apprenticeship and study. To photograph a sailing ship the operator must have a knowledge of seamanship, he must be able to detect sails that are setting badly, gear that is out of place, and to direct the ship to the most suitable course for lighting. Given favourable weather conditions we can guarantee a successful result, modern lenses and speedy shutters defying the fastest speed boat. A yacht under sail should always afford as many opportunities as possible to the operator, often a lull in the breeze causes her to stand upright at the moment of exposure, or she sails into the wind causing a flutter in the jib topsail. There should be three main positions manœuvered for, lee bow, lee broadside and lee quarter. Where possible these positions should be arranged for beforehand. The lighting should cross the headsails, rounding off the curves and throwing the mainsail into relief. The lighting is most important and should never be full on the sails as it accentuates the small creases and bulges caused by the battens. The vessel should not be sailed too close to the wind but allowed to gather as much way as possible and it is imperative when approaching the operator to set a straight course and hold to it, allowing the operator to make his own distance of which he must be the best judge.

Yacht & Marine Photos
List by Beken & Son, Cowes,
Isle of Wight, 1928

Introduction

by Bob Fisher

'If she looks right, she'll go right' was how an old salt gave me early instruction in yacht design. He then devoted many hours to telling me what 'looked right'. I was lucky. I spent my childhood in the small Essex yachting and fishing village of Brightlingsea, where many of the men around the waterside wore Guernsey jumpers bearing the names of the famous yachts of the 1920s and 1930s; *Shamrock* and *Endeavour* were common among them, and indeed some of these yachtsmen had been among those who went on strike — for pay to compensate their loss of a season's fishing — aboard Sir T.O.M.Sopwith's America's Cup challenger in 1934. It was a place redolent with their stories and in me they had a willing listener.

I soon began to understand the mysteries of why some boats were always better than others and why some were never likely to do well. It was a doctrine which clouded my understanding for quite some time, as these men discounted the human element in assessing a yacht's performance, with the notable exception that they held that the amateur had no place in a racing yacht. 'Any fool can pull a sheet,' they would say, and add, 'but it takes a seaman to ease one.' There is still some truth in that, but today there is far greater regard for the effect of the crew on a racing yacht. They can transform a boat beyond belief, as Harold Cudmore and his crew did to *Phoenix* in 1985, although they will still need the basic raw material of success, a boat which has the ability to match the performance of her competitors, a thoroughbred.

Since I first became interested in yachts, the design — both of cruising boats and of those which race — has changed considerably, and I am sure that same old salt might take some time to agree that the fast boats of today do 'look right', yet perhaps there is a gradual return to the shapes that he would acknowledge to be correct. High freeboards, reverse sheer and stunted overhangs stayed for a long period and brought with them a hardly acceptable functional ugliness, for yachts should have grace, they should 'look right'. They are the pleasure pursuits of their owners and, while not all of these owners may be blessed with aestheticism, they are aware that their boats should stand out in the fleet through performance or beauty.

It would have taken much to make the earlier generations admit that functional design had its place, and a reference to *Shamrock IV*, Sir Thomas Lipton's 'ugly duckling' (the words are those of her designer, Charles E. Nicholson), being his best challenger for the America's Cup would have been shrugged off. Yet that very functional yacht, of which Alfred F. Loomis wrote, 'She looks something like a cross between a tortoise and an armoured cruiser,' provided Lipton with his race wins in the Cup. The old salts, among them Tom Diaper, were scathing of the crew of *Shamrock IV*, and objected in particular that she had too many amateur sailing masters. Diaper insisted, 'I could pick 35 men now, and have only one gentleman to take the time, and a Yankee to represent America, and to see fair play, with myself in command. I would sail *Shamrock IV*, and I tell you I would beat the *Resolute*.' Paradoxically, *Resolute* had Charles Francis Adams as her skipper, another amateur!

There are many like Tom Diaper today and, in the rapidly changing climate at the upper end of the yacht-racing strata, a few are capable of producing notably better performances. Those who can are those who pay the greatest attention to detail. Whether my erstwhile tutor would appreciate the graphics which now adorn most yachts is doubtful. For him, yachts were white or occasionally black; for

13

Porto Cervo, Sardinia

Opposite:
Kialoa IV (see page 85)

Sir Thomas Lipton they were green. Their decoration would have been restricted to the gold leaf of the caveta line with some scroll-work at its ends, possibly reflecting the name of the yacht. Each morning their decks would have been scrubbed, and the holystoning would take place weekly; the brightwork would be chamoised off and the brass polished gleamingly before breakfast in those days when, to owners, quality was largely skin-deep.

Today the broad splashes of colour are as the warpaint of the Red Indian — an announcement of a yacht's prowess, and a ready identification of the owner. The racing machine has no concession to comfort, with the barest of accommodation (to comply with the rating rules) since the demands are such that every man's weight is best distributed on deck and feeding is for afterwards. I doubt the old salts would have approved of that; they lived aboard, ate well and worked hard.

What the change has wrought is boats that are more efficient, yachts which are faster and more handy to manoeuvre and a breed that spends more time out of the water than it does afloat. They are none the worse for that at a time when there is a distinct lack of mooring space throughout the world. Many years ago one owner apparently proved that it was cheaper to 'dry sail' his ocean racer than it was to keep her in a marina berth; the rest now slavishly follow suit without counting the

14

cost, for it has long been appreciated that if you have to ask 'How much?' in the world of yachting, you cannot afford to race yachts.

The new breed is more seaworthy, and those who howled to the contrary after the 1979 Fastnet Race were ill-informed. Those who have been to sea in a yacht of the 1940s or earlier will readily appreciate that her modern counterpart — which floats on the water rather than *in it* — is ultimately a safer prospect when winds reach the top of the Beaufort scale. No longer are there tragic stories of yachts being overwhelmed by seas and sinking; even those which suffer quite considerable damage manage to find their way home, despite the harder way that they are driven. The lesson of the 1979 Fastnet was that one should stay with the boat rather than take to a liferaft — the maxim for that should be that one steps up into a liferaft rather than climbs down into it. For where in the past there have been races won by yachtsmen who have ridden out storms behind headlands, the modern yacht is expected to go to windward in any wind. Uncomfortable it may be, but the yachts are more capable, and their crews prepared to try.

Yacht racing, even cruising, is not all battling with the elements; it is utilizing them to one's own advantage, and the better the design and construction of the yacht, the better the ultimate result can be.

After a period of rapid improvement in the 1970s, there came a period of consolidation in the early 1980s, largely a result of the constraints of various racing rules. Then came a few milestones, like Ben Lexcen's breakthrough in the 12-Metres, a class which was rapidly becoming almost one-design until the advent of the winged keel. Now the Twelves are developing diversely and sophisticatedly a rule which was devised in 1906. Other rules are exploited by designers while the rulemakers plug the holes they open; it is a game of providence and persistence on the one hand and of petulance and pragmatism on the other. The game has reached the stage where one side has opted to examine fresh ideas. A new breed of boats, both racing and cruising, is being developed without the restrictive clauses of any racing rule, while naval architects are able to advance their theories on making fast and weatherly yachts; it is perhaps the beginning of a new Golden Age of yacht design.

And all the while the cameras of the Beken family record the changing face of yachting, not only in that sailing Mecca, Cowes, but throughout the world where

English Harbour, Antigua

Victoria Harbour, Canada

the sport gives pleasure. It is a pertinent record, and one which, because of its originators, is authoritative. There is very little missed in the recording of images by the Bekens, as all too many of us who have been caught at a moment we would prefer to forget will bear witness, and they treat the beauty of the yachts in a manner calculated to enhance them.

The excellence of the Bekens' photography is recognized all over the world. It was no surprise to me to find their work adorning the walls of the Norfolk Hotel, the sailors' watering-hole in Fremantle. It has decorated royal palaces and seedy houses of ill-repute in Bangkok; it is an art form all of its own. Beken photographs are as recognizable as the boats they capture; their quality has been around for a century, and has become as much a part of the sport as yachting itself.

Kookaburra III

Iain Murray, it is reliably reported, approached the Alan Bond syndicate to see if it needed his talents as a skipper for the 26th Defence of the America's Cup. He had, after all, worked with them in the final stages of their preparation in Newport, after his *Advance* had been eliminated, as helmsman of *Challenge 12*, the other eliminated Australian boat which had become *Australia II*'s trial horse. Murray says the invitation never came, but all the while he had other plans.

He encouraged Kevin Parry into financing a second Western Australian syndicate; one whose budget Parry allowed to develop like Topsy from an initial A$6 millions to one which finally exceeded A$25 millions. It was a syndicate which came close to success, and which gave Parry sufficient confidence to provide finance again for a challenge to return the America's Cup to Fremantle.

Murray was more to the Parry syndicate than just a skipper; he was project director and co-designer, with John Swarbrick, of all three *Kookaburra*s. He has a mathematical mind and the ability to absorb all facets of technology. Murray was the leading light in the research which was carried out at the National Ship Model Basin at Wageningen in Holland, and it was he who recruited the experts in their fields to form the most powerful 12-Metre camp in Australia — just a stone's throw along Mews Road, Fremantle, from where Alan Bond had his.

There was never much between the last two *Kookaburra*s; *Kookaburra II* was even fitted with a new keel just before the Cup races and trialled against *Kookaburra III* to see if she was faster; and it may have been that Murray missed a step forward at the last to match Dennis Conner. Suffice to say, *Kookaburra III* beat *Australia IV* by 5−0 in a best-of-nine race series to pick the Cup defender. Then when she met *Stars & Stripes* she also met her end; the scoreline was 4−0 and the average margin a minute and a half; the golden-hulled Twelve was just not good enough to repulse the invader.

Name of yacht:−	KOOKABURRA III
Registered:	Australia 1986
Owner:	Taskforce '87 Ltd/Parry Corp. Ltd.
Skipper:	Iain Murray
Designer:	Murray & Swarbrick Yacht Design
Builder:	Parry Boatbuilders
Materials:	Aluminium
Launched:	1986
Length o/a:	20.5 metres
Length w/l:	14.0 metres
Beam:	3.70 metres
Draft:	2.70 metres
Displacement:	26,000 kilos
Rating:	12 Metre class
Sails by:	North/Sobstad
Sail area:	166 sq.metres

America II and KZ 3

Name of yacht:—	AMERICA II
Registered:	United States 1986
Owner:	America II Syndicate
Skipper:	John Kolius
Designer:	Sparkman & Stephens
Builder:	Williams & Manchester
Materials:	Lt. Alloy
Launched:	1986
Length o/a:	19.81 metres (65ft)
Length w/l:	14.02 metres (46ft)
Beam:	3.81 metres (12ft 6in)
Draft:	2.74 metres (9ft)
Displacement:	28,349 kilos (63,785 lb)
Rating:	12 Metre class
Sails by:	Various
Sail area:	162.575 sq.metres (1,749 sq.ft)

America II — this one is US 42 — is a series of three boats designed by the Madison Avenue naval architects Sparkman & Stephens, under the direction of Bill Langan. All three were built in aluminium by Williams and Manchester at Newport, Rhode Island, in an endeavour to return the America's Cup to that octagonal room in the New York Yacht Club where it stood for 132 years until it was plundered by the men from 'down under'.

The NYYC team spent all the possible sailing hours off Fremantle, knowing well that to practise in the waters where the Cup races would be held made sense; after all, hadn't there been the continual moan from previous challengers that the Americans held all the aces because of their local knowledge? Perhaps because of this they were able to show competitiveness in the 12-Metre World Championship a year before the Cup races were due to be held on the same waters; *America II* finished third and, but for two human foul-ups, could have won.

KZ 3 was the world's first glass-fibre Twelve, and the secret of her hull was kept almost until the launching day by building her in conjunction with the internationally renowned firm of McMullen and Wing in Auckland, whose prowess in aluminium construction was famous. The 'plastic fantastics' were designed by the combined talents of Bruce Farr (rig), Laurie Davidson (hull) and Ron Holland (keel) and showed a fresh and imaginative attitude; the boats were noticeably beamier than any of their predecessors, a feature clear in comparison with *America II*.

Condor of Bermuda

This maxi yacht was designed by John Sharp and built in wood by Emsworth Shipyard for the 1977—78 Whitbread Round the World Race, in which she was jointly skippered by Robin Knox-Johnston and Leslie Williams. Financed by Bob Bell and sponsored by C.E. Heath insurance brokers, she became, at the eleventh hour, *Heath's Condor* for the race. This was a name which gave great confusion to the foreign yachting writers who sought to associate it with Britain's former yachting prime minister.

Just before the name-change came a change of mast — a carbon fibre spar replaced the aluminium one with only three days to go to the start of race. The untried nature of this operation was to backfire on her crew when the mast collapsed during the first leg and *Heath's Condor* made an unscheduled stop in Monrovia, a halt which put paid to the chances of winning and to the health of most of the crew.

Bell took over when the boat returned to Britain after completing the Whitbread race and began to campaign her around the international maxi-circuit, breaking the course record in the storm-struck 1979 Fastnet Race. It was during that race, on the leg back from the Scilly Islands, that *Condor* broached, turning to face the way she had come. The boat staggered to her feet and stood head to wind with the spinnaker all over the spreaders. Peter Blake, who happened to be steering *Condor* at the time, felt her begin to make a stern board, so he reversed the helm until she was facing the way he wanted her to and the sails began to fill — the spinnaker almost explosively — so that she charged off in the direction of Plymouth!

Condor was then sailed out to Sydney, where she took part in the Sydney to Hobart Race and then on to McMullen and Wing's yard in Auckland for the first of her massive refits. It was on the way back across the Pacific that she was wrecked on a lonely atoll, then salvaged and rebuilt at the Auckland yard with many modifications to her bow, stern and keel before resuming her place in the maxi-circuit.

Condor has now retired from racing and her owner, Bob Bell, has had her converted for luxury cruising.

Name of yacht: – CONDOR OF BERMUDA	
Registered:	Bermuda 1979
Owner:	R. Bell
Skipper:	R. Bell
Designer:	J. Sharp
Builder:	Emsworth Shipyard
Materials:	Wood
Launched:	1977
Length o/a:	23.5 metres (77ft)
Length w/l:	19.5 metres (64ft)
Beam:	5.60 metres (18 ft 4in)
Draft:	3.20 metres (10ft 6in)
Displacement:	39,626 kilos (87,296 lb)
Rating:	64 feet IOR
Sails by:	Butler Verner

Lion New Zealand

Name of yacht: – LION NEW ZEALAND	
Registered:	New Zealand 1985
Owner:	P. Blake & Associates
Skipper:	P. Blake
Designer:	R. Holland
Builder:	T. Gurr
Materials:	Kevlar/Balsa
Launched:	1984
Length o/a:	23.59 metres
Length w/l:	19.96 metres
Beam:	5.51 metres
Draft:	4.18 metres
Displacement:	35,024 kilos
Rating:	68.6 feet IOR
Sails by:	Hood
Sail area:	295 sq.metres

'Loins', as she was affectionately known to her crew, was Peter Blake's fourth vehicle for the Whitbread Round the World Race. He approached Ron Holland to design the boat for the 1985–86 event, knowing that his fellow-New Zealander was the leading designer of maxi-boats at that time and that he had already completed most of a similar project for the same race for the late Rob James.

Blake was convinced that the race would be won by the boat whose crew pushed it hardest, perhaps remembering the time when, in the previous race, he had pushed *Ceramco New Zealand* past the bigger *Flyer* shortly after rounding Cape Horn by means of continual sail changes. In 1985 he took 17, three more than the other maxis, but in that race the conditions did not warrant the bigger crew and Blake had to be content with second place in his brewery-sponsored boat, *Lion New Zealand*.

Condor (with Lion New Zealand)

The differences between a 'grand prix' maxi-rater and a similar-sized boat built specifically to win the Whitbread Round the World Race are small but specific. The two types rarely race together and it is only once every four years that there is any real opportunity for them to do so — when the circumnavigators meet in England prior to the start of the world event, at which time they usually take part in the Channel and Fastnet Races. It is rarer still for two maxis of these different types from the same designer to stretch out together but it happened for Ron Holland in the 1985 Channel Race when *Lion New Zealand* met *Condor*.

Condor was the boat which Bob Bell commissioned to replace his earlier boat of the same name on the maxi-circuit. She was coloured a deep plum and was built in Penryn using the latest in high-technology plastics — combining Kevlar and carbon fibres — by a team assembled specially for the purpose.

The 80-footer has had a long and successful racing career, including scooping the pool in the 1983 Fastnet Race when she was not only first home in a new record time (taking the record from *Condor of Bermuda*) but was also the corrected time winner. The Fastnet Cup was full to overflowing for Bell and his crew in Plymouth.

Many of the world's top sailors have raced on board *Condor*, including Dennis Conner who had the embarrassment of putting her aground, on Hampstead Ledge, when leading the final race of the 1981 Seahorse Maxi Series. *Condor* was stuck fast on a falling tide and, despite some complex and even confused attempts to get her off to continue the race, she was only refloated by the use of her engine. The awful moments were recorded for posterity on film for television and, according to producer Jeremy Pallant, a record number of sound-edits had to be made to protect delicate ears!

Name of yacht:–	CONDOR
Registered:	Bermuda 1985
Owner:	R. Bell
Skipper:	R. Bell
Designer:	R. Holland
Builder:	Mid Ocean Marine
Materials:	Kevlar/Carbon/S-Glass
Launched:	1981
Length o/a:	24.48 metres (80ft 4in)
Beam:	5.68 metres (18ft 8in)
Draft:	3.97 metres (13ft)
Displacement:	34,437 kilos (75,865 lb)
Rating:	70 feet IOR
Sails by:	North/Sobstad
Sail area:	316 sq.metres (3,401 sq. feet)

Amazing Grace

Name of yacht:–	AMAZING GRACE
Registered:	Canada 1985
Owner:	R. Herron
Skipper:	R. Herron
Designer:	C. & C.
Builder:	C. & C.
Materials:	Kevlar/Balsa/Nomex
Launched:	1980
Length o/a:	13.61 metres (44ft 8in)
Length w/l:	11.21 metres (36ft 9in)
Beam:	4.10 metres (13ft 5in)
Draft:	2.62 metres (8ft 7in)
Displacement:	9,304 kilos (20,511 lb)
Rating:	33.8 feet IOR
Sails by:	Hood
Sail area:	105.5 sq.metres (1,135 sq.ft)

A 45-footer designed by Cuthbertson and Cassian, *Amazing Grace* is typical of the type of boat which has developed within the limitations of the International Offshore Rule. Short-ended and beamy, these boats utilize the parameters of a complex rule to provide seaworthy yachts able to race within a handicap system.

Amazing Grace has provided her owner, Roger Herron, with what is by contemporary standards a long racing life. She was launched from C. and C. Custom yard in June 1980, campaigned in major events that year and in the early Florida spring for the Admiral's Cup, an event in which she has become something of a veteran; after her 1981 appearance she returned for the following two Admiral's Cups.

This photograph was taken during the 1985 Admiral's Cup, on a day of brisk breeze and on a point of sailing where these masthead-rigged boats are slightly disadvantaged, relying upon a basically unstable spinnaker for much of their power. The crew of *Amazing Grace* have used a No. 4 genoa, set on the headstay, instead of a more usual staysail inside the spinnaker. In these conditions it is almost certainly the headsail which will be used to go upwind, probably with a reef in the mainsail.

Antares

Philippe Briand designed *Antares* as a 'pocket maxi' in 1981, a size of boat which provides many of the thrills of the bigger boats and which, because of the complexities of handicapping from the IOR, can often beat the 70-ft raters on corrected time. *Antares* proved this when she won the Seahorse Maxi Series in her first season.

Briand was considered to be highly innovative in designing this size of yacht with a fractional rig. At the time anything bigger than a One-Tonner used a masthead rig, but Briand put considerable effort into the spar-design technology for *Antares*, believing the rig to be the most controllable in fresh winds, the sort of conditions in which she is revelling here.

Close reaching using a double-head rig, *Antares* is producing for skipper Yves Pajot the easily steerable ride which Briand had defined. The harmony of the rig is enhanced by setting the small staysail in the 'slot' between the Solent jib and the mainsail to encourage a fast airflow. This is even more important in rough sea conditions than in the flat water of the Solent on this black day during *Antares'* successful Seahorse Series.

Name of yacht:—	ANTARES
Registered:	France 1981
Skipper:	Y. Pajot
Designer:	P. Briand
Builder:	Chantier Laguen & Hemidy
Materials:	Aluminium
Launched:	1981
Length o/a:	19.00 metres
Beam:	5.00 metres
Displacement:	18,000 kilos
Rating:	53 feet IOR
Sails by:	Hood
Sail area:	240 sq.metres

Apricot

Name of yacht:–	APRICOT
Registered:	United Kingdom 1985
Owner:	A. Bullimore
Skipper:	A. Bullimore
Designer:	N. Irens
Builder:	N. Irens
Materials:	Kevlar/Carbon/Epoxy
Launched:	1985
Length o/a:	18.28 metres
Length w/l:	18.00 metres
Beam:	12.80 metres
Draft:	2.75 metres/1 metre
Displacement:	5,000 kilos
Rating:	Formula II multihull
Sails by:	Hood
Sail area:	200 sq.metres

Tony Bullimore commissioned the design and building of this 60-ft trimaran from Nigel Irens. She was constructed from the latest high-tech plastics, Kevlar and carbon fibres in an epoxy mix, in order to be both light and strong: there is nothing which slows a multihull more than weight, unless it be a lack of stiffness to support the rig.

Irens' determination during the construction resulted in an instantly fast boat, one aimed primarily at shorthanded racing but geared also for fast passage races with a small crew (the space below limited the numbers for a long period).

The first success came very early on in her life when, with Bullimore as skipper and Irens as crew, *Apricot* won the 1985 Round Britain Race. The race was one with a mixed bag of weather, and there were sufficiently strong winds to eliminate some of her less well designed and constructed opponents.

Apricot was totally dominant in the 1985 TAG Round Europe Race, winning each of the eight legs in Class 2, and success followed success for her as Irens worked with Bullimore to refine her rig — probably one of the simplest wing-mast rigs ever seen on an offshore multihull. It too was designed and built by Irens, using similar plastics technology to the hull structure, and was far superior to the extruded aluminium spars of her rivals.

Her life came to a sudden end during the 1986 Route du Rhum, when she was returning to France shortly after the start with a smashed port hull. She had hit some floating wreckage during a period when the winds had reached Force 9, and was returning to Brest. *Apricot* went on to the rocks less than a mile from the harbour, where she foundered. Skipper Tony Bullimore saved himself by the simple expedient of diving into the sea, clambering over the rocks and up the cliff-face to safety.

In 1987 the transatlantic west-east sailing record, from the Ambrose Light at New York to the Lizard in Cornwall, is held by Philippe Poupon's 75-ft Irens trimaran *Fleury Michon*. She is a development of *Apricot*, bearing a strong visual resemblance, and achieved the crossing in 7 days 12 hours and 50 minutes; 3,130 miles at an average speed of 17.28 knots.

Admiral's Cup

The biennial Admiral's Cup attracts teams from all over the world. During Cowes Week, three boats per country contest a series of five races — three inshore and two offshore. The inshore events make quite a spectacle, consisting of courses in the Solent and, since 1983, Olympic triangle-style circuits in nearby Christchurch Bay. The offshore events are the Channel Race and the Fastnet.

With a large number of One-Tonners taking part in the Admiral's Cup in 1985 (hardly surprising, as the event followed hard on the heels of the One Ton Cup at Poole), it might have been expected that, in the inshore races, there would be some confusion around the marks; crowding at the very least.

In the pictures opposite and overleaf the crew of *Diva* (S99) have not helped themselves by dropping the spinnaker in the water. As the sail fills with water it will slow the boat dramatically. *Justine IV* (IR 290) may have found some difficulty in keeping clear, particularly if *Espace du Désir* (F85) continues as aggressively as she is here.

The scene is symptomatic of the changes which are gradually occurring in the sport due to the intense competition in the level-rating championships, particularly the One Ton Cup, and now this is making the overall standard more uniformly high. Collisions are rare, however....

When they do happen there is something of an inevitability about it all.

The Solent is full of traps, which the locals know well to avoid. Those who don't know and understand its trickery can all too easily be caught out. This time it is the tide at Frigate, just off the Beaulieu shore, which has trapped the unwary.

Eric Duchemin, in *Fiere Lady* (F9119), has paid the penalty of not establishing, and claiming, his overlap at the mark in sufficient time; the tide has brought all those to leeward up rapidly and the gap has closed. It has closed so fast for *Fiere Lady* that she has been forced to gybe and that has put her on port tack.

The Dutch boat *Mustang* (H63) has even more of the blame to bear, for her crew too should have seen it beginning to happen and taken avoiding action. Once again the position is that the group of One-Tonners, similarly rated boats, are bound to go at much the same speed, and therefore arrive at marks in close proximity. It is incidents like these (or, more properly, the avoidance of them) which mark out the great from the not so great.

Atlantic Privateer

Name of yacht:– ATLANTIC PRIVATEER	
Registered:	United States 1985
Owner:	P. Kuttel
Skipper:	P. Kuttel
Designer:	B. Farr & Associates
Builder:	Round the World Yachts PTY
Materials:	Kevlar/Nomex/Aluminium
Launched:	1984
Length o/a:	24.32 metres (79ft 9in)
Length w/l:	19.40 metres (63ft 8in)
Beam:	5.56 metres (18ft 3in)
Draft:	3.88 metres (12ft 9in)
Displacement:	30,332 kilos (66,810 lb)
Rating:	69.5ft IOR
Sails by:	Hood
Sail area:	284.5 sq.metres (3,062 sq.feet)

There was always a dark cloud over *Atlantic Privateer*, a boat which promised much and fulfilled rather less. She was designed by Bruce Farr to win the 1985–86 Whitbread Round the World Race for Padda Kuttel, and was built in Cape Town. Sponsorship from the computer giant Apple Macintosh saw that name on the side of the boat in her early career.

At the end of the Cape Town–Punta del Este race some unpleasantness ashore resulted in the withdrawal of that sponsorship and the name-change to *Atlantic Privateer* as an unsponsored entry in the Whitbread. Prior to the 29,000-mile classic, the 80-footer began to produce some impressive performances, notably in the Seahorse Maxi Series and in the Fastnet Race, where she came within a whisker of being the new record-holder after finishing a close second to *Nirvana*.

At the start of the Whitbread, *Atlantic Privateer* was favourite to win. Kuttel had chosen a tough crew, including three of those who had completed the race with him in *Xargo III* four years earlier. It is a race, however, which penalizes false economy, and the penalty was brought home to *Atlantic Privateer* when she was almost within sight of her home port and leading the race comfortably.

The mast was the one which *Flyer* had used four years earlier to win the Whitbread race, and which was scheduled to have been replaced before the 1985/86 race began. It wasn't, and it folded as she crashed into huge seas as she beat into the South East Trades. A new mast was stepped after she had retired from the leg and, after the most exciting finish with *NZI Enterprise*, she won the next leg into Auckland. From then on she never seemed to be able to repeat that type of performance and added bad choice of course to her other failings on the remaining legs.

Australia II

Australia II changed the face of yachting history: her 41-second win in the final race of the 1983 America's Cup ended the longest winning streak in the annals of sport. The 'Little White Pointer' carved her way through opposition on the water and ashore to realize Alan Bond's ambition to take the Cup to Perth.

Designed by Ben Lexcen, *Australia II* held the best-kept secret of the docksides until an hour or so after her Cup win. Bond lifted both his arms and the skirt which shrouded her keel was cast aside and the world saw the 'magic' winged keel for the first time. This was the keel which almost brought the America's Cup to a standstill before a race took place.

Australia II was designed with the aid of the tank-testing facilities at the National Ship Model Basin in Holland where, it was alleged, scientists took a more than academic interest in the project and gave input contrary to the conditions governing the America's Cup in the eyes of the New York Yacht Club. The ensuing battle over this was known as the Keelgate Affair and kept both sides busy for two months.

Australia II was very different from the 12- Metres of her day in other aspects. She was small and much of her underbody aft of the keel was cut away giving her a tight turning circle — the perfect match-racing Twelve. Her 'fighter' reputation caused several rival skippers to defer to her at the pre-starts and allow John Bertrand to choose where he wanted to start.

Australia II formed the base of the Bond syndicate's operation in the early stages of the defence campaign and the boats which Lexcen subsequently designed were developments of her. Her last competitive sailing was in the 1986 12-Metre World Championship, in which she finished fourth.

Australia II's days afloat ended when she was bought by the Australian government to be preserved as a museum exhibit.

Name of yacht:–	AUSTRALIA II
Registered:	Australia 1986
Owner:	A.Bond
Skipper:	G.Lucas
Designer:	Ben Lexcen
Builder:	S. Ward
Materials:	Aluminium
Launched:	1982
Rating:	12 Metre class
Sails by:	North/Sobstad

Awesome

Name of yacht:–	AWESOME
Registered:	United States of America 1981
Owner:	W.Zimerli
Skipper:	W.Zimerli
Designer:	B.Chance
Builder:	New Orleans Marine/Derector
Materials:	GRP
Launched:	1973
Length o/a:	13.8 metres (45ft 3in)
Length w/l:	12.2 metres (40ft)
Beam:	3.73 metres (12ft 3in)
Draft: 2.70 metres/1.42 metres (8ft 10in/4ft 8in)	
Displacement:	11,884 kilos (26,180 lb)
Rating:	37.2 feet IOR
Sails by:	North
Sail area:	86 sq.metres (926 sq.feet)

Britton Chance Jr is often referred to as the *enfant terrible* of yacht design, a wayward, well-connected talent whose results are at opposite ends of the success spectrum. An early exponent of the testing tanks with a mathematical scientist's view of naval architecture, Chance eliminates the unnecessary from his designs.

Chance's approach — of which *Awesome* is a prime example — is to have hull shapes which create the minimum of drag, and to that end he exploits the light-displacement, narrow-beam type of hull which is extremely fast downwind, but which has limitations in the upwind performance. Chance uses centreboards to help to minimize the Achilles heel and, with the original owner of *Awesome*, Bill Snaith (she was then called *Figaro*, like all Snaith's yachts), was commissioned by an understanding owner who was prepared to give the designer his head.

Earlier two-masters, like *Equation*, provided Chance with a fine base for this 45-footer which he says is Bill Snaith's legacy to yachting, although due to ill-health he was not able to campaign her as he would have liked. Her name was changed to *Rhumbrunner* when she was purchased by Buddy Friedrichs, and in his hands she became the scourge of the Gulf Coast offshore racing fleet.

With yet another new name, *Awesome*, she changed hands again and was bought by Will Zimerli. He took her to Antigua in 1981, to conditions where she was bound to show well (and rate similarly under the handicap system used in the Islands). In this photograph she thunders along on a broad reach with everything pulling and leaves very little wake to show for it.

Acadia and Obsession

Name of yacht:–	ACADIA
Registered:	United Stated of America 1980
Owner:	B. Keenan
Designer:	G. Frers
Builder:	Minneford
Materials:	Aluminium
Launched:	1978
Length o/a:	15.55 metres (51ft)
Length w/l:	12.56 metres (41ft 2in)
Beam:	4.44 metres (14ft 7in)
Draft:	2.57 metres (8ft 5in)
Displacement:	14,813 kilos (32,633 lb)
Rating:	39.1 feet IOR
Sails by:	North/Hood
Sail area:	114.46 sq.metres (1,232 sq.feet)

In 1980 the Sardinia Cup was held for the second time; the first had been guarantee enough for a good turnout. It was a series with mixed weather, but no one who was there will ever forget the run home from the Iles de Porqueroles in the long race, a mistral-hit race which had one of the smallest boats winning by two hours on corrected time, because her crew had had the courage to hoist a spinnaker while the rest kept theirs below decks.

Acadia had won the SORC convincingly earlier in the year and formed part of the victorious American team at Porto Cervo. She was one of the earliest of the *Serendipity* 43s designed by Doug Peterson, and she was built in glass-fibre by New Orleans Marine for Burt Keenan. Her crew knew every wrinkle in order to get the best from her.

In this picture, *Acadia* has locked into the stern wave of *Obsession* (designed by Sparkman & Stephens), a boat rating almost two feet higher which had been chartered for the Canadian team. The smaller boat was able to hang on to this 'tow' all the way down this leg and the next after a better gybe at the wing mark, thus scoring a noticeable gain.

Congere

One never dares ask American yachtsmen why they come to England to race, and because of that one never really knows what it is that attracts them to Cowes like moths to a candle flame. Like those moths, they almost invariably are scorched, if not burned. Certainly that was the case for Bevin Koeppel and his latest *Congere*, and whether he made the transatlantic crossing for Cowes Week or to compete in the 1985 Fastnet, one can never be quite sure. *Congere* had some trouble keeping her hull under her mast during the blowy races of Cowes Week that year (when this picture was taken) and made Plymouth, but not by way of the Fastnet Rock, in the 'classic'.

But then there are many underlying questions one might want to ask about the boat because she does not seem to fit into any category; she stands almost unique among the thoroughbreds of today because of her size: 61 ft overall. Designed by German Frers, the aluminium *Congere* is markedly bigger than the group racing around 40 ft rating and not big enough to be a 'mini-maxi'. Very few IOR boats are built at this size, and those few are generally aimed at the Whitbread Round the World Race, yet it is a size which can provide the owners with a modicum of comfort even in a boat which has racing as her main aim. *Congere* has an owner's cabin aft, even if some lightening of the cockpit had to be made to cope with the extra weight.

One of the races which *Congere*'s owner finds attractive is the Buenos Aires – Rio de Janeiro, and one can hardly blame him for that. *Congere* held the record for the race until, in 1987, the former *Ondine* beat her home to take the best elapsed time ever. During that race, sailmaker Butch Ulmer became 'Butch the Broach' for steering *Congere* into a broach of gigantic proportions. However, she maintained slightly more than a 10-knots average, but when she arrived in Rio the Americans in her crew, owner included, were threatened with deportation because they did not have the correct visas for the country!

Name of yacht:–	CONGERE
Registered:	United States of America 1985
Owner:	B. Koeppel
Skipper:	B. Koeppel
Designer:	G. Frers
Builder:	Palmer Johnson
Materials:	Aluminium
Launched:	1983
Length o/a:	18.87 metres (61ft 11in)
Length w/l:	15.43 metres (50ft 7in)
Beam:	5.18 metres (17ft)
Draft:	3.30 metres (10ft 10in)
Displacement:	18,801 kilos (41,419 lb)
Rating:	51.4 feet IOR
Sails by:	Ulmer/Kolius
Sail area:	163.23 sq.metres (1,757 sq.feet)

Backlash

Name of yacht:–	BACKLASH
Registered:	United Kingdom 1985
Owner:	T. & C. Herring
Skipper:	T. Herring
Designer:	J. Everitt
Builder:	Vision Yachts
Materials:	Kevlar/Carbon/Epoxy/Foam
Launched:	1985
Length o/a:	13.04 metres
Length w/l:	9.91 metres
Beam:	3.81 metres
Draft:	2.22 metres
Displacement:	7,484 kilos
Rating:	33.5 feet IOR
Sails by:	Banks/Sobstad/McWilliams
Sail area:	96.9 sq.metres

When Tim and Cathy Herring went to Julian Everitt for an Admiral's Cup design they were prepared to give the naval architect a free hand and to be adventurous with his interpretation of the IOR. They were also prepared to allow the results to come slowly at first and to develop the boat somewhat empirically.

In addition, the Herrings wanted to race the boat all over the world, and were not prepared to miss a trick to improve the boat's performance, even if this meant keel changes. Everitt was convinced that the canard type keel was worth all the penalties which it would bring under the rule but in her first season *Backlash* was sailed mostly with a conventional keel as the Herrings preferred to begin with a conservative approach. *Backlash* was built in Cowes by Vision Yachts, of a high-tech mix with Kevlar, carbon fibre and epoxy resin. If she lacked anything, it was in stability, and she benefited enormously from an extra few crew on her rail, as in this Cowes Week picture. It was here in 1985 that she really shone, including among her wins the highly prestigious Britannia Cup.

Winter was spent on the far side of the Atlantic, where after sailing across on her own bottom *Backlash* competed in the SORC and Antigua Race Week before the Herrings sailed her back to begin racing on Britain's south coast again. It was then that the canard made its appearance on a regular basis. A new keel with a laminar flow bulb sticking forward of the foil was complemented by a centreboard-type canard which was lifted when not hard on the breeze to reduce wetted surface area. A relatively successful Cowes Week in 1986 was followed by a trophy-stripping exercise in the Herrings' home-based Burnham Week, in which they won the Town Cup, the Week's Points Trophy and several other prizes.

Barracuda of Tarrant

'Star' of a BBC television serial (*Howards' Way*), *Barracuda of Tarrant* is a 45-ft Ultra Light Displacement Boat designed by Tony Castro to the express requirements of Bob Fisher. The Californian ULDBs had pointed a way which the owner wished to exploit even further by using beam aft to increase stability so that the boat could be cruised, fast, with a small amount of people in the crew.

Continuing the maximum beam almost all the way aft, with underwater sections not unlike those of the Flying Dutchman, gave Castro the opportunity to use twin rudders angled outward so that when the hull is heeled the leeward rudder is fully immersed and vertical. That has made the steering as near-perfect as possible, and broaching in heavy weather with a spinnaker rare enough not to have to be considered. This makes the boat a viable shorthanded fast cruiser.

The hull, of three skins of cedar, became, first of all, the plug for a glass-fibre mould for the production version by Sadlers of Poole, while the deck is the first glass-reinforced plastic moulding from that yard. *Barracuda of Tarrant* was built, 200 years after HMS *Elephant*, at the same site at Bursledon in Hampshire by the Elephant Boatyard — the yard where the television programme was filmed.

In this high-class soap opera *Barracuda* helped the mythical yard out of bankruptcy and was sailed across the Atlantic single-handed by the fictional designer's daughter.

In real life she has established herself as a character in cruising and racing, making her first passage (to race in Scotland) of 585 miles in 72 hours. She was the fastest monohull in the 1986 Round the Island Race, and only ten minutes outside the 73-ft *Mistress Quickly*'s all-time record of 5 hours 57 minutes. She was also a regular line honours winner in Channel Handicap class races — the designer's brief was to forget totally the IOR — and collected several corrected time prizes as well, both for inshore and in the longer offshore races.

Barracuda of Tarrant was Yacht of the Year in the Silk Cut Nautical Awards for 1987.

Name of yacht: – BARRACUDA of TARRANT	
Registered:	United Kingdom 1986
Owner:	B. Fisher
Skipper:	B. Fisher
Designer:	A. Castro
Builder:	Elephant Boatyard
Materials:	Cedar/Spruce/Epoxy
Launched:	1986
Length o/a:	13.70 metres
Length w/l:	12.80 metres
Beam:	3.80 metres
Draft:	2.40 metres
Displacement:	5,672 kilos
Rating:	1.154 Channel Handicap
Sails by:	Sobstad
Sail area:	87.8 sq.metres

Blizzard

Name of yacht:–	BLIZZARD
Registered:	United Kingdom 1979
Owner:	E. Juer
Skipper:	E. Juer
Designer:	G. Frers
Builder:	Palmer Johnson
Materials:	Aluminium
Launched:	1979
Length o/a:	15.52 metres
Length w/l:	12.56 metres
Beam:	4.40 metres
Draft:	2.59 metres
Displacement:	9,198 kilos
Rating:	39.6 feet IOR
Sails by:	North
Sail area:	145.9 sq.metres

When Ernest Juer commissioned a new 'Admiral's Cupper' from German Frers he made several logical steps. The choice of Frers for a Class I boat for the competition was expedient at the time, since it was this designer who was monopolizing the results with this size of boat (and continued to do so for many years).

The choice of material and the builder were incontrovertibly linked. For a 51-footer, aluminium undoubtedly held all the best options at this time. And aluminium boat-building for racing craft was the province of Palmer Johnson of Sturgeon Bay, Wisconsin. Their position, in America's heartland, gave rise to the name of the yacht; she emerged from her builder's shed into a snow-storm.

The first race was to get Blizzard to the SORC in Florida, which Juer saw as an ideal racing shakedown prior to an Admiral's Cup trial season in Britain. That early racing proved invaluable.

As soon as the trials began there was little doubt that Blizzard was going to be selected. Juer had forged around him a top-class crew with Tom Richardson behind the wheel and Bobby Lowein as navigator. The Cup races of 1979 began with a resounding victory for Blizzard; line honours and corrected time winner by four minutes. The brisk breezes and the strong spring tides in the Solent had worked together in Blizzard's favour, and thus it might have been expected that with brisker breezes and stronger tides she might have repeated that win the following day.

But, as Sir Max Aitken once said of sailing: 'A fellow can have an off-day.' Blizzard's crew had all of theirs together. Not only did some of the boat's gear let them down but a series of minor errors led to one major navigational disaster. Blizzard rounded Salt Mead buoy, more than halfway through the race, with a lead big enough to save her time, and headed back up the Solent instead of crossing to West Lepe. In doing so she threw the race away.

Sadly, it is for that mistake, rather than all her race wins, that Blizzard will be remembered.

Azzurra II

Name of yacht:–	AZZURRA II
Registered:	Italy 1986
Owner:	Consorzio Azzurra Sfida Italiana
	America's Cup 1987
Skipper:	L. Bortolotti
Designer:	A.Vallicelli
Builder:	S.A.I. Ambrosini Shipyards
Materials:	Aluminium
Launched:	1985
Length o/a:	20.05 metres
Length w/l:	13.9 metres
Beam:	3.85 metres
Draft:	2.85 metres
Displacement:	26,000 kilos
Rating:	12 Metre class
Sails by:	North
Sail area:	168 sq.metres

The good showing by the Yacht Club Costa Smeralda syndicate at its first attempt in the America's Cup in 1983 hardened its resolve to be the challenger for 1987. Andrea Vallicelli (who designed *Azzurra*, which had reached the challenger semi-finals in Newport) was commissioned to design her successor, a boat to cope with the stronger wind conditions found off Fremantle.

The need for such a boat was all the more obvious following the world championship in her home waters. In that she was beaten by *Victory '83*, recently purchased by the rival Yacht Club Italiano syndicate. When this syndicate (headed by the Aga Khan) does anything, it does it with style, and the whole *Azzurra* campaign was handled in that way.

Azzurra II was the first of three new boats, and the syndicate spent the 'down under' summers testing their boats in the Cup waters. They proved, beyond any measure of doubt, that you cannot win the America's Cup simply by throwing money at it, even if you do have designers and builders of international repute. And it needs more than talent; cohesion and co-operation are equally necessary ingredients for success.

Drum

There was an overlying sadness with *Drum* which seemed to pervade her campaign to win the 1985—86 Whitbread Round the World Race. The untimely death of Rob James (drowned off the trimaran *Colt Cars GB*) began an unhappy series of chapters for *Drum*. The Ron Holland design was originally for James and his Japanese car-manufacturer sponsor; it was taken up by them and then stopped in mid-construction when there was a change of top management within Mitsubishi.

The part-built boat was bought by Michael and Paul Berrow with Simon le Bon, and they found the nucleus of her builders at Vision Yachts in Cowes, who agreed to complete the construction while Moodys, at Swanwick, began to prefabricate the interior. Skip Novak became the project manager, the boat came together within a tight time schedule and for a while all looked good.

This picture was taken on a blowy day during the Seahorse Maxi Series with Harold Cudmore calling the shots over Novak's shoulder. That series should have been an almost sufficient test of boat and gear, but when *Drum* took part in the Fastnet Race she had an accident which no one could have foreseen. The aluminium matrix above the lead of her keel had been incorrectly welded and it broke, leaving the boat with no ballast. She instantly capsized. The rescue operation included diving to remove six crew members trapped in the upturned but buoyant hull, but it was quickly achieved.

Drum was salvaged, and Moodys carried out a miraculous rebuild to have her ready for the start of the race. Then during the first leg her hull began to delaminate badly in the same heavy winds that took *Atlantic Privateer*'s mast. Novak had to ease up, and lost three days limping into Cape Town for what proved to be yet another major rebuild.

Drum completed the race in third place and took part in another circumnavigation in the summer of 1986, this time the less hazardous one around Ireland.

Name of yacht:—	DRUM
Registered:	United Kingdom 1985
Owner:	Simon Le Bon & P.& M. Berrow
Skipper:	Skip Novak
Designer:	R. Holland
Builder:	Mitsubishi Marine/Vision Yachts
Materials:	GRP/Kevlar/Foam
Launched:	1985
Length o/a:	23.6 metres
Length w/l:	18.4 metres
Beam:	5.4 metres
Draft:	4.14 metres
Displacement:	34,331 kilos
Rating:	69.4 feet IOR
Sails by:	Hood
Sail area:	297 sq.metres

Blue Buzzard

Blue Buzzard was built, as *Uin-na-Mara*, by Supercraft in Hong Kong as one of a pair for the Colony's Admiral's Cup team; her sister ship was *Vanguard*, owned by David Lieu. Kevlar, a relative rarity in 1979, was included in the plastic lay-up of these boats and they formed, with Chris Ostenfeld's *La Pantera III*, a powerful team.

It was hardly surprising, therefore, that when the first day's racing in the Admiral's Cup was over Hong Kong led the points table, eleven clear of Britain, whose *Blizzard* had come first. The three Hong Kong boats stacked the placings from 3rd to 5th, with *Uin-na-Mara* the middle one of them. The team stayed on top after the next race, but the Channel Race, with lighter winds, proved its undoing. Hong Kong nevertheless finished third, equal with Italy, in 1979 — the year of the stormy Fastnet.

Uin-na-Mara returned to the same fray two years later, but then the Hong Kong team, although it had the same skippers, was not as strong as it had been on the previous occasion. For *Uin-na-Mara* it was not the last occasion in which she would be involved in the event. Two years later, under her new owner, Martin Gibson, and her new name, *Blue Buzzard*, she was back, contending for a place in the British team, albeit unsuccessfully.

Name of yacht:–	BLUE BUZZARD
Registered:	United Kingdom 1984
Owner:	M. Gibson
Skipper:	M. Gibson
Designer:	E. Dubois
Builder:	Supercraft
Materials:	GRP/Kevlar
Launched:	1979
Length o/a:	13.61 metres
Length w/l:	10.67 metres
Beam:	3.95 metres
Draft:	2.41 metres
Displacement:	9,135 kilos
Rating:	35.8 feet IOR
Sails by:	Pryde/Horizon
Sail area:	108.26 sq.metres

Blue Leopard

Name of yacht:–	° BLUE LEOPARD
Registered:	United Kingdom 1974
Owner:	D. Molins
Skipper:	D. Molins
Designer:	Laurent Giles
Builder:	W. Osborne
Materials:	Wood
Launched:	1962
Length o/a:	33.99 metres
Length w/l:	22.86 metres
Beam:	5.79 metres
Draft:	2.90 metres
Displacement:	69,650 kilos
Sails by:	Ratsey & Lapthorn
Sail area:	325.15 sq.metres

No yacht could be more of an ocean thoroughbred than *Blue Leopard*, although she was built strictly for cruising. When she was constructed, by William Osborne and Company in 1962, she was the biggest new yacht of her time; nothing of this size had been built since prewar days.

Designed by Laurent Giles and Partners, *Blue Leopard* provided them with a challenge; that of creating a motor-sailer that was uncompromising in every way. The fact that the company was able to meet this challenge was favourably noticed by *Yachting World* in its review of the boat: 'She is, without question, the most successful combination of fully-rigged sailing yacht, fast motor yacht and comfortable home afloat ever produced.' To further endorse the designers' prowess, her original owner, Desmond Molins, retains her twenty-five years later.

Blue Leopard was very much a light-displacement design in an age when very few boats of this type were considered, let alone built. Osborne's built her using two skins of Honduras mahogany sandwiching two of diagonally laid American cedar. The deck is effectively a box of two plywood layers separated by spruce stringers and foam; a method of construction well ahead of its time. It means that she displaces 50 tons when light and just over 60 when fully equipped for cruising.

Blue Leopard has spent the majority of her life in the Mediterranean, and is capable of 11 knots to windward and 15 knots when reaching, topping 16 knots broad reaching under sail and power in an effortless manner, as befits a yacht with two 380 hp Rolls-Royce turbocharged diesels, and whose hull was tank-tested at the Stevens Institute in Hoboken, New Jersey, where many of the 12-Metres and the J-class *Ranger* were tested.

Blue Leopard is constantly updated by her owner, and remains the envy of many. A request to the designers for another yacht to the same pattern had to be turned down since the original contract protects *Blue Leopard*'s unique design.

Brava

Pasquale Landolfi is one of Italy's most competitive ocean racers and has a long track record of Admiral's Cup racing. His previous *Brava*, another Vallicelli design, had been one of the top scorers in the 1983 Cup races and, had Italy had a third boat of the calibre of her and *Almagores*, the Cup might have found a new home. In what was principally a bonanza for the minimum-rated boats, *Brava*, rating 34.2ft, finished in equal third place with *Pinta* behind *Almagores* and *Sabina*, each of whom were just three points ahead.

Landolfi had taken three seasons to work *Brava* up to her full potential. He turned again to Andrea Vallicelli for his next boat and, with the Admiral's Cup in mind, it had to be a One-Tonner. Fast One-Tonners are fractionally rigged, and this meant a whole new conceptual change for Landolfi and his always highly competent crew.

For the new *Brava* he went to Morri and Para in Rimini, who built the hull in wood, and capped this with a composite deck. She was completed early in 1984 and was one of Italy's Sardinia Cup team, finishing third overall. By the following year she was well worked up for the Admiral's Cup and was quite easily the best of the, admittedly weak, Italian team.

Here in that Admiral's Cup she displays the joy of a lightish-displacement One-Tonner in a fresh breeze. The ability to plane makes this size of modern offshore racer an exciting boat. *Brava* is using full main and has kept her No. 3, a Solent jib, set underneath her biggest (1.5 ounce) nylon spinnaker.

Name of yacht:–	BRAVA
Registered:	Italy 1985
Owner:	P. Landolfi
Skipper:	P. Landolfi
Designer:	A. Vallicelli
Builder:	Morri & Para
Materials:	Wood/Composite
Launched:	1984
Length o/a:	12.20 metres
Length w/l:	9.80 metres
Beam:	3.75 metres
Draft:	2.25 metres
Displacement:	5,583 kilos
Rating:	30.5 feet IOR
Sails by:	North
Sail area:	78.28 sq.metres

Cider with Rosie

Name of yacht:–	CIDER WITH ROSIE
Registered:	United Kingdom 1978
Owner:	N. Svendsen
Designer:	G. Frers
Builder:	Frers & Cibillis
Materials:	GRP/Foam
Launched:	1974
Length o/a:	11.76 metres
Length w/l:	8.99 metres
Beam:	3.49 metres
Draft:	1.97 metres
Displacement:	7,128 kilos
Rating:	27 feet IOR
Sails by:	Ratsey & Lapthorn
Sail area:	77.47 sq.metres

There are moments in a helmsman's life when he wishes it would all go away… and this is one of them. *Cider with Rosie* is a 1974 vintage Frers One-Tonner (back in the days when the One Ton limit was 27.5 ft IOR), and at that time all her type had a tendency to take control on the downwind legs in brisk breezes. Every helmsman, if he is honest, would admit that he has experienced this near-terminal experience. For this is the moment of truth, like standing in your suit of lights before the bull, the banderillas sticking out of its neck, when all hell is about to break loose.

The broach has been averted by winding on lots of rudder, but that resulted in the over-correction which is about to turn *Cider with Rosie* into the type of picnic through which the bull has charged. At any moment the mainsail, already by the lee, is about to take up its rightful position relative to the wind; the boom is arcing dangerously across the deck and *Rosie* will be pinned down on her starboard side as she twists wildly to face the way she came. It's then that the helmsman seriously thinks of taking up golf.

Formidable

One might suppose that this helmsman was brave enough to think that he had everything under control. Peter Vroon could fool you into that most of the time, and as this squall hit *Formidable* he does appear to be in slightly better shape than the boats to windward of him. The day was that now infamous Thursday of the 1979 Cowes Week when the Solent gave notice of the Fastnet Race to come.

That day sails were ripped to shreds, masts tumbled and rudders shattered into shards as the sou'wester tore across the sheltered waters. It was a day to be remembered, one of which every helmsman, every crewman, has a tale to tell.

What Vroon had was a boat which seemed to dominate the racing scene year after year. As *Marionette*, she had been Chris Dunning's captain's boat in a successful Admiral's Cup team and the following year, in Vroon's hands, she had won the Channel Race by 12 hours on corrected time, a race in which she was just ahead of the calm which left most competitors stuck at the notorious CH1 buoy off Cherbourg, or in deluging rain in mid-Channel later.

What might just tip the scales in Vroon's favour on this occasion is if he can get the boat to bear away a touch. His crew have set him up for it; the spinnaker has been eased and the mainsail let right out, but a touch less downhaul on the boom vang would have been even more helpful. What might tip the balance (and the boat) against him is the fact that the boom end is already in the water.

Vroon went on to take this boat, which had been built in aluminium by the Joyce brothers, to a series of successes for another couple of seasons, making her a reference point in similar-sized boats for Ron Holland.

Name of yacht:—	FORMIDABLE
Registered:	Holland 1979
Owner:	P. Vroon
Skipper:	P. Vroon
Designer:	R. Holland
Builder:	Joyce Marine
Materials:	Aluminium
Launched:	1977
Length o/a:	14.5 metres
Beam:	4.5 metres
Draft:	2.42 metres
Displacement:	9,979 kilos
Rating:	34.5 feet IOR
Sails by:	North
Sail area:	136 sq.metres

Caiman II

Name of yacht:–	CAIMAN II
Registered:	Holland 1985
Owner:	G. Jeelof
Skipper:	G. Jeelof
Designer:	D. Peterson
Builder:	J. Rogers
Materials:	Kevlar/Foam
Launched:	1981
Length o/a:	12.94 metres
Beam:	3.88 metres
Draft:	2.45 metres
Displacement:	7,903 kilos
Rating:	32.9 feet IOR
Sails by:	North

A boat with great staying power, *Caiman II* saw competition in three Admiral's Cups. She was designed by Doug Peterson in a classic period and built by Jeremy Rogers' custom division at the same time as *Apollo V* and *Marionette VIII*, using vacuum-bag techniques to bond the epoxy/Kevlar mix on to unicellular foam.

When Gerry Jeelof was based in England, he campaigned for the British team and, when he failed to make the side in the first season, 1981, he chartered to the Bermudans. The first inshore was not one that many people will remember with a great deal of pleasure. Jeelof will, however, as Jay Hooper steered *Caiman II* in the light airs and strong spring tides on the day of the Royal Wedding to be first home, and winner too on corrected time. No one would forget that if he owned the boat.

The rest of that Cup series is probably best forgotten, as Bermuda finished last and *Caiman II* came out of the team to do the Fastnet as a non-Admiral's Cup entry. Two years later, back in Holland, Jeelof contested his own country's Cup trials and emerged with *Caiman II* as top boat. Then in the Cup races *Caiman II* failed, like so many others; she failed to produce what she had promised, and was the lowest points scorer in the Dutch team.

Caiman II was back again in 1985 when she was top scorer for the Dutch, but this was a poor team which threw away many chances, and *Caiman II* was beginning to show her age. It was not long before she made way for a newer boat, but on this day in her last series she was obviously still giving much pleasure to those on board.

Carat

Another classic Frers 50 that seemingly did not age, *Carat* gave her owner, Wictor Forss, a boat with which he campaigned around the world at the major regattas. She was a regular at the SORC and the Sardinia Cup, as well as the Admiral's Cup. Built by Minnefords in the United States, *Carat* was constructed in aluminium to replace Forss' *Bla Carat*.

She was launched towards the end of 1981, but it was in 1983 that she made her Admiral's Cup debut, and on a never-to-be-forgotten day marked a triumph for her owner and crew. There were many reasons for people to remember that day. For the purist, it was the first inshore race in the Cup that was held outside the Solent; for the observer, the black storm-clouds blotted out the sky in the middle of the race; and Forss and the crew of *Carat* will remember well the race itself.

They would have wanted to forget the windless Channel Race when the fleet arrived at the CH 1 buoy off Cherbourg as the ebb began and they waited for six hours before they could lift their anchors and start racing again. The third inshore race in Christchurch Bay was a totally different affair, despite the barbed lightning which flashed occasionally. Nothing could dampen the spirits on *Carat*.

The race committee set a perfect line for the start, and it was little wonder that the pecking order became established almost exactly in descending order of IOR ratings. *Carat* was out in front in the first mile, and there she stayed around the 30-mile Olympic-style course, to win the race on corrected time. The win brought the Champagne Mumm Trophy and the owner's weight in the sponsor's product — 50 bottles of it, sufficient to make this a memorable day for Wictor Forss.

Name of yacht:—	CARAT
Registered:	Sweden 1985
Owner:	W. Forss
Designer:	G.Frers
Builder:	Minneford
Materials:	Aluminium
Launched:	1981
Length o/a:	15.45 metres
Beam:	4.45 metres
Draft:	2.85 metres
Displacement:	13,452 kilos
Rating:	40 feet IOR
Sails by:	Sobstad
Sail area:	142.75 sq.metres

Ceramco New Zealand

Name of yacht: – CERAMCO NEW ZEALAND	
Registered:	New Zealand 1981
Skipper:	P.Blake
Designer:	B.Farr
Builder:	McMullen & Wing
Materials:	Aluminium
Launched:	1980
Length o/a:	20.88 metres
Length w/l:	16.80 metres
Beam:	5.20 metres
Draft:	3.24 metres
Displacement:	19.320 kilos
Rating:	62.9 feet IOR
Sails by:	Lidgard Rudling

This is the story of what might have been, a fairy-tale story which went wrong and saw skipper Peter Blake with crippling damage in his third Whitbread Round the World Race in a row. The first time it was the hull of *Burton Cutter* that failed; next it was the carbon fibre mast of *Heath's Condor* that collapsed; and this time it was a similar failure on *Ceramco* that robbed Blake of the overall win in the 1981–82 race.

After the second Whitbread race had stopped at Auckland there was the possibility of a boat for Blake, fully sponsored, to compete in the next race. The seed was sown as Blake arrived as watch captain to skipper Robin Knox-Johnston, the line honours winner, into his home port. It took the businesslike approach of Tom Clarke to provide the underwriting for the boat through Ceramco, one of New Zealand's largest corporations.

Public support for the venture was always there, and it was to be an all-Kiwi effort; Bruce Farr drew the lines of the 68-ft fractional rigger and she was built, of aluminium, by the Auckland yard of McMullen and Wing. Freeze-dried food and a desalinator reduced the all-up weight of the boat and she went about a series of rigorous tests before sailing to the start of the big race.

One of those tests was to compete in the 1980 Sydney to Hobart race. The race records show that it was won by *New Zealand*; because of IYRU Rule 26 regarding sponsorship the *Ceramco* had to be dropped, but everyone back in New Zealand knew which boat it was. Blake and his crew claimed a rare line honours and corrected time double in a tough race. *Ceramco New Zealand* had passed her tests with flying colours.

There was no doubt whatsoever when she started the race from Portsmouth that *Ceramco New Zealand* was the favourite, but 120 miles north of Ascension Island the failure of a rod shroud where it went over the spreader resulted in the mast collapsing, and the yacht took a round trip of 4,000 miles to sail the 2,500 to Cape Town under jury rig. With a new mast she won the leg to Auckland, and her subsequent performance showed that, had the first mast stayed in, there would have been a different name on the Whitbread Trophy in 1982.

Côte d'Or

Name of yacht:–	COTE D'OR
Registered:	Belgium 1985
Owner:	Côte D'Or Co.
Skipper:	E.Tabarly
Designer:	Joubert & Nivelt
Builder:	Amtec/Willebroeck
Materials:	Kevlar/Divinycell
Launched:	1985
Length o/a:	25.10 metres
Length w/l:	20.3 metres
Beam:	5.9 metres
Draft:	3.9 metres
Displacement:	33,987 kilos
Rating:	69.6 feet IOR
Sails by :	North
Sail area:	249 sq.metres

At 82 ft the biggest boat in the 1985–86 Whitbread Race, *Côte d'Or* was built in Belgium of composite sandwich for Eric Tabarly's fourth attempt to win this blue-water race. Unfortunately for Tabarly, the money to build this Joubert/Nivelt design came too late. The construction was rushed, the boat untried, and the combination nearly proved fatal.

Belgium's famous chocolatier put up the money for the maxi-racer, and at first insisted that all the crew be Belgian. Slowly Tabarly insinuated more and more of the Frenchmen he knew would be able to handle this type of boat, and

the proportion of Belgians on board was under 50 per cent by the time the race started.

The lateness of the project showed up in the first leg when hammering to windward in big seas; the forward sections of the hull began to delaminate. They did so again in the floor on the second leg, and there were huge rebuilds at both Cape Town and Auckland. Then on the final leg *Côte d'Or* showed her true potential when she finished second to *UBS Switzerland* and in reaching conditions pulled away from the other maxis.

Intrigue, Drake's Prayer and Challenge III

For her Admiral's Cup team of 1985, Australia provided three very different boats from three different designers, with two owners who were totally new to the event. 'Lou has finally won his Guernsey' was how one Australian ocean-racer described the choice of Lou Abrahams and *Challenge III* for the Admiral's Cup team after nearly a quarter-century of trying. His Frers-designed, masthead-rigged 43-footer made third place in the Australian trials, but a broken mast in the Channel Race pulled her down in the points scoring. She was, however, ready for the next race.

Sir Francis Drake's daily prayer to his Maker makes reference to finishing started business; therefore the name was an apposite follow-on to Peter Kurts' *Once More Dear Friends*. This time he changed designers, to Bruce Farr, for a fractionally rigged 43-footer similar to *Snake Oil*, which had performed so well in the SORC. Then, as usual for Peter Kurts, he packed the boat with talented sailors.

Star-class gold medallist David Forbes shared the wheel with Iain Murray, the six-times 18-ft Skiff world champion who was the nominated skipper of the Kookaburra 12-Metre syndicate, for what was Kurts' third attempt to win the Admiral's Cup. Conditions for the series tended to favour the One-Tonners, and particularly so in the Channel Race where the course was 90 per cent reaching in strong winds.

While *Drake's Prayer* had finally headed the Australian selection trials, it was Don Calvert's *Intrigue* which had dominated racing, and she qualified for the team without having to complete the long final race. Don's father had built another Admiral's Cupper, in an apple shed, just a mile away from where Don built his *Intrigue* to the design of Tony Castro. The earlier boat was the *Caprice of Huon* (designed by Robert Clark), which in Sydneysiders' hands had helped Australia to its first Cup win. *Intrigue*, however, was the first Tasmanian boat and crew to be selected for an Australian team. It was not to be a winning team, but *Intrigue* was to be its top points scorer.

Name of yacht:—	INTRIGUE
Registered:	Australia 1985
Owner:	D.Calvert
Skipper:	D.Calvert
Designer:	A.Castro
Builder:	Wilson & Goode
Materials:	Wood/Epoxy
Launched:	1984
Length o/a:	12.21 metres
Beam:	3.98 metres
Draft:	2.18 metres
Displacement:	5,869 kilos
Rating:	30.3 feet IOR
Sails by:	North
Sail area:	78.46 sq.metres

Challenger

Name of yacht:–	CHALLENGER
Registered:	United Kingdom 1983
Owner:	L.Williams
Skipper:	L.Williams
Designer:	D.Peterson/D.Allan-Williams
Builder:	Southern Ocean Shipyards
Materials:	GRP
Launched:	1980
Length o/a:	24.26 metres
Length w/l:	20.72 metres
Beam:	6.10 metres
Draft:	3.84 metres
Displacement:	34,546 kilos
Rating:	68.8 feet IOR
Sails by:	Hood
Sail area:	262 sq.metres

'Come out and give me a hand with the boat this afternoon,' said Les Williams. 'I've a few guests coming on board, and I don't think they'll be trimming the sails.' The afternoon in question was a day in Cowes Week 1983, when this picture was taken, and the invitation came as a result of my sailing more than 2,000 miles in *Challenger* double-handed with Les. The guests in question turned out to be Princess Alexandra — who had launched the yacht — and her husband Angus Ogilvy, who were staying on board *Britannia*.

It was one of the good days in the strife-torn life of this maxi-rater. She was a boat which promised so much and just failed to deliver, for a multiplicity of reasons. Designed jointly by David Allan-Williams and Doug Peterson, *Challenger* was built in glass-reinforced plastics by Southern Ocean Shipyards of Poole as the first of their Ocean 80s. Originally named *Ocean Greyhound* (following sponsorship from the bus company), she sailed in the Round the Island Race of 1980, shortly after her launch.

She was then fractionally rigged, and because of her incompleteness she could only set a reefed mainsail, down to the hounds, yet was still only one minute outside the record established for the race by *Mistress Quickly*. Certainly she had the speed potential, but somehow it was never completely realized, probably because her sail wardrobe was never fully maintained.

In her first year she sailed to the United States, and almost lost her mast in Hurricane George. The following year, now called *FCF Challenger*, she took part in the Whitbread Round the World Race and lost her mast with just a thousand miles to go. She finished under jury rig. A new masthead-rigged spar was stepped and, as *Stevens Lefield Challenger*, she took part in the 1982 Round Britain Race and then went for a year's charter work in the Caribbean. In September 1983, her career ended abruptly when a series of financial disputes saw her hauled out of the water at Swanwick, near Southampton.

Charles Heidsieck III

Alain Gabbay was the bright-faced young sailor who surprised the racing world when he won the second leg of the 1977—78 Whitbread Round the World Race with *33 Export*, a boat noted for not suffering from an over-indulgence in maintenance. That win ensured for him major sponsorship for the next race four years later, one which brought him to the start of the race with *Charles Heidsieck III*, a new, well-prepared boat which was capable of winning the race on corrected time.

Gilles Vaton designed the 64-ft boat to be capable of just that and there was no compromise to comfort; down below there was no standing headroom and only the off-watch crew had bunks — the sails took up much of the space and they were regarded as being of greater importance!

Gabbay took great care to take his champagne-sponsored boat to the competition before the main event, using the name *Champagne Charlie* to avoid protest under Rule 26. He took on the best in the SORC and then went on the maxi-boat circuit in America where it became patently obvious that this was a boat which would give a good account of herself in any company, and one which would revel in the more boisterous conditions which prevail in the Southern Ocean. Chantier Pouvreau had constructed her strongly but lightly in aluminium, and did so before the 'planing flap' at the stern was penalized. Just prior to the Whitbread race, *Charles Heidsieck III* was entered for the Two-handed Transatlantic Race and finished third of the monohulls and ninth overall.

In the Whitbread things appeared to be running well. She surprised everyone by being second to finish in Cape Town and was in the same place on corrected time, a state of affairs which remained at the halfway stage in Auckland. When the small boats dominated the third leg it was *Charles Heidsieck III* which went to the top of the overall standings, leading *Kriter IX* by 11 hours and *Flyer* by 34 on corrected time. It seemed that there was nothing more to do but to cover her French rival to the finish to take the top place. But Gabbay made the mistake of not paying enough attention to what *Flyer* did in front and was caught out by the North Atlantic High, finishing 30 hours behind *Flyer* on corrected time; so close, and yet…

Name of yacht:– CHARLES HEIDSIECK III	
Registered:	France 1981
Owner:	Charlie Ocean
Skipper:	A. Gabbay
Designer:	G. Vaton
Builder:	Pouvreau
Materials:	Aluminium
Launched:	1980
Length o/a:	20.30 metres
Length w/l:	16.40 metres
Beam:	4.74 metres
Draft:	3.30 metres
Displacement:	20,190 kilos
Rating:	54.4 feet IOR
Sails by:	Hood
Sail area:	183 sq.metres

Chrismi II

Name of yacht:—	CHRISMI II
Registered:	United States 1982
Designer:	M. Francis
Builder:	Trehard Constructions Navales
Materials:	Aluminium
Launched:	1981
Length o/a:	26.0 metres (85ft 4in)
Length w/l:	21.5 metres (70ft 6in)
Beam:	5.8 metres (19ft)
Draft:	3.75 metres (12ft 4in)
Displacement:	60,000 kilos (132,180 lb)
Sails by:	Hood
Sail area:	364 sq.metres (3,918 sq.feet)

When the rating rules are thrown out of the window, yacht designers have the opportunity to express themselves by producing fast, seaworthy sailing boats, yet one always feels that those rating rules retain an influence because of the way that they have directed past thinking in naval architecture. With *Chrismi II* Martin Francis accepted the challenge to design a fast yacht whose prime use would be for charter.

This 85-footer combines speed with luxury. Down below there are six double cabins, each with its separate head and shower — charterers are becoming more hedonistic and less spartan in their attitude to time spent afloat. They want the feel of the traditional mahogany interior but they want it with cushioned comfort.

Chrismi II meets all those needs; she is redolent of luxury, and yet she retains the performance of an ocean-racing thoroughbred. Francis ensured that performance would not be lost when he specified aluminium for her construction at Christian Trehard's yard at Biot, near Antibes in France. It was Trehard's initial specification to which Francis worked on this project.

The yacht caused quite a sensation when she made her first appearance in the West Indies. Her first appearance in Antigua was as the winner of the Guadeloupe–Antigua race, and it is off that tropical island that this picture was taken as she competed in Antigua Race Week — that strange combination of races which links a series of parties.

Chrismi II and her sister ship, *Concorde*, were designed for charter in the West Indies in the winter and in the Greek Islands in the summer. Each year, therefore, they have two Atlantic crossings between their charter seasons.

Disque d'Or 3

Name of yacht:	DISQUE D'OR 3
Registered:	Switzerland 1980
Owner:	P. Fehlmann
Skipper:	P. Fehlmann
Designer:	B. Farr
Builder:	Pouvreau
Materials:	Aluminium
Launched:	1980
Length o/a:	17.78 metres
Length w/l:	13.75 metres
Beam:	5.04 metres
Draft:	2.76 metres
Displacement:	14,176 kilos
Rating:	46.6 feet IOR
Sails by:	Hood

This was the third in a series of boats to bear this name and be skippered by Pierre Fehlmann, that most meticulous of ocean racers. Fehlmann went to Bruce Farr for the design of this 58-footer to take part in the 1981–82 Whitbread Round the World Race. He aimed at the highly competitive handicap prize, believing that to be best with a boat of this size — a fact which has been borne out in practice in three of the four races.

In order to prepare for that circumnavigation, Fehlmann sought some competition in other ocean races and included in his schedule the SORC and Antigua Race Week; his was to be a thoroughly prepared programme. Unfortunately for him, the boat was over-built to withstand the rigours of the Southern Ocean. The original light-displacement concept of *Disque d'Or 3* was partially lost as a result, and she finished fourth.

She competed in yet another round-the-world race, the BOC Around Alone, skippered by South African Bertie Reed and under the sponsor's name as *Stabilo Boss*.

Kialoa IV

Many is the port which has rocked with the red-shirted figures of *Kialoa*'s crew. Jim Kilroy's crew race hard and play hard and are the most peripatetic of the maxi-raters. Wherever there was a big race, *Kialoa IV* was there. And that is only in the past tense because, to maintain his competitive edge, Jim Kilroy has pensioned off *Kialoa IV* in favour of his new *Kialoa V*, designed by German Frers.

Kialoa IV was the first of a new breed of maxi-raters, more than 80 ft long, and was designed by Ron Holland to be built using composite plastics. She also followed Holland's space-frame concept of putting a chassis inside the boat to take the keel and rig stresses, highly important in a maxi where these loadings are extremely heavy. *Kialoa IV* was built by Holland's brother-in-law, Gary Carlin, at his Kiwi Yachts yard in Florida. She had been designed after the Fastnet Race of 1979 and was launched in the November of the following year.

Immediately Jim Kilroy began a working-up session for the new boat which involved her trialling against her predecessor, a boat which he was to convert later for cruising. It was probably the first time since Sir T.O.M. Sopwith that an owner had two significantly large racing yachts where the latter could be assessed against the former, a boat of known performance.

This assessment was a technique which had a significant effect on the early performance of *Kialoa IV*; she went straight into the fray and won races, although it has to be admitted that there was something erratic about her earliest performances. However, by mid-season she was more than good enough to win the Seahorse Maxi Series, which included a race over the original America's Cup course. From then on she was the scourge of the world maxi-circuit for the best part of three years, and her owner was not averse to the more light-hearted regattas, like Antigua Race Week where this picture was taken.

Name of yacht:–	KIALOA IV
Registered:	United States of America 1982
Owner:	J. Kilroy
Skipper:	J. Kilroy
Designer:	R. Holland
Builder:	Kiwi Boats
Materials:	GRP/Kevlar
Launched:	1980
Length o/a:	24.48 metres (80ft 4in)
Length w/l:	19.29 metres (63ft 3in)
Beam:	5.65 metres (18ft 6in)
Draft:	3.79 metres (12ft 5in)
Displacement:	35,652 kilos (78,541 lb)
Rating:	69.6 feet IOR
Sails by:	Hood
Sail area:	262.9 sq.metres (2,830 sq.feet)

Colt International

Colt International shed the first part of her name to comply with the International Yacht Racing Rule 26 (which relates to sponsorship), in order to compete in the 1985 Seahorse Maxi Series at Cowes and the Fastnet. They were all part of her shakedown for what her owner considered to be the serious event, the following year's Carlsberg Two-handed Transatlantic Race.

She has competed with distinction in the SORC and the Royal Ocean Racing Club's race to the Caribbean but it was the shorthanded event for which she was built and lovingly prepared. She started with an advantage, in that she was built by Nautor, a Swan 59, designed by German Frers and constructed in 'bulletproof'-style glass-fibre. The rigours of the North Atlantic were unlikely to concern her.

Colt International was let down by her self-steering gear, which failed early in the transatlantic race, but she did sufficiently well to lead the 60-ft monohull class until 400 miles from the finish, when she was overtaken by two of the specialist boats built for this type of racing.

Fourteen of these Swan 59s have been produced, principally as cruising yachts, with a centreboard version available for those who wish to add cruising in shoal waters to their itinerary. Like all Swans, they are concessionless in their luxury, which leads one to wonder just how *Colt International* did so well, a standard production boat against the top custom-built opposition.

Name of yacht:–	COLT INTERNATIONAL
Registered:	Finland 1985
Owner:	Ocean Racing OY.
Designer:	G.Frers
Builder:	Nautor
Materials:	GRP/Foam
Launched:	1984
Length o/a:	18.38 metres
Length w/l:	14.69 metres
Beam:	4.99 metres
Draft:	3.40 metres
Displacement:	21,732 kilos
Rating:	44.7 feet IOR
Sail area:	155.75 sq.metres

New Zealand 7

Name of yacht:–	NEW ZEALAND 7
Registered:	New Zealand 1986
Owner:	BNZ America's Cup Challenge
Skipper:	C. Dickson
Designer:	
B. Farr/R. Holland/L. Davidson/R. Bowler	
Builder:	
McMullen & Wing/Marten Marine Industries	
Materials:	GRP
Length o/a:	19.5 metres
Length w/l:	14.1 metres
Beam:	3.95 metres
Draft:	2.70 metres
Rating:	12 Metre class
Sails by:	
North/Hood/Sobstad/Lidgard/In house	

There are more sailmakers per capita in New Zealand than anywhere else in the world. That statistic must mean that they are either incredibly non-productive or, more likely, that there are a greater percentage of sailors in the Land of the Long White Cloud than in any other country. Auckland is known as the City of Sails, and while the New Zealand Challenge for the America's Cup originated in that city, it had the whole country of three and a half million people behind it in no time.

New Zealand 7 was a huge success story. The nationalistic urge was sufficient to encourage the top three Kiwi designers (some will say the three best in the world), Laurie Davidson, Bruce Farr and Ron Holland, to combine their talents. The result was phenomenal. In the 12-Metre World Championship one of their glass-fibre prototypes, *New Zealand 5*, finished second and that did much to aid the fund-raising in the home country.

The third glass-fibre Twelve was a refinement of the two earlier boats with the knowledge of the few months' sailing which the two had had together and the experience gained from the championship. In the new boat was a crew that was second to none, even Dennis Conner's, and a skipper with the 'steel-blue eyes of a U-boat Commander', as British newspaper journalist Ian Wooldridge saw fit to describe Chris Dickson.

For most of the summer they were almost invincible. In the three round-robins only Conner was able to beat them and they started the semi-finals with a 33 wins, 1 loss record. The way in which the Kiwis demolished *French Kiss* was almost unseemly; 4−0 and only once did the French get ahead. *New Zealand 7* had boat-speed to spare.

The axe fell when they met the executioner in the challenger final, for the Louis Vuitton Cup. It was not to be totally one-sided; *New Zealand 7* did win the third of this best of seven race series, pouncing on a gear failure on *Stars & Stripes* to go ahead by the second mark and staying there to the finish after a record number of 55 tacks on the final beat, but generally Conner had the upper hand.

Container

Udo Schütz built this 32.3 rating offshore boat in an attempt to make the German Admiral's Cup team in 1983. He failed when a trio of One-Tonners not only dominated the German trials but went on to win the Cup itself. He suffered the same fate in 1985, but this *Container* — one of a series of Schütz's boats to bear the name — was part of the successful German team in the Sardinia Cup in 1984, and as consolation was in the Austrian (generally known as the German second XI) team in both the Admiral's Cups.

Container's 'first team' choice for Germany, however, saw her in a winning team by the narrowest of margins; a mere half-point. The margin would have been considerably greater if the German team had observed the prime rule of racing in this type of competition, that of staying out of trouble, and particularly staying out of the protest room. It was not *Container* (skippered by Uli Libor) that got herself into trouble but her sister ship, *Pinta*.

Pinta hit the Hugh Welbourn *Panda* at the gybe mark in the final race of the series and, when found guilty by the International Jury, received a 20 per cent points penalty. When that decision was announced it put Italy into a half-point lead over Germany, but the following protest saw the Papua New Guinea team yacht, *Super Schtroumph*, also penalized 20 per cent. The subsequent place shifting gave *Pinta* an extra point and the Germans the Sardinia Cup to add to the Admiral's Cup which they had won a year earlier. And that protest against *Pinta* might not even have been heard because *Panda* flew her protest flag inferior to the racing flag on her backstay and not superior as the sailing instructions demanded. It took Lawrie Smith, *Panda*'s helmsman, to point out that the IYRU rules state that Code Flag B is always acceptable, irrespective of any other provisions in the sailing instructions.

On that fateful day the skippers of *Container* and *Pinta* had had a gentlemen's agreement to stay clear of each other and not race for the individual points prize until the last leg. *Pinta*'s infraction put that in the lap of Libor and *Container*.

Name of yacht:–	CONTAINER
Registered:	Germany 1985
Owner:	U. Schütz
Skipper:	U. Libor
Designer:	Judel/Vrolijk
Builder:	Schutz Werke
Materials:	Kevlar/Carbon/Honeycomb
Launched:	1983
Length o/a:	12.95 metres
Beam:	4.11 metres
Draft:	2.40 metres
Displacement:	7,298 kilos
Rating:	32 feet IOR
Sails by:	North
Sail area:	94.81 sq.metres

Italia

Name of yacht:–	ITALIA
Registered:	Italy 1986
Owner:	Consorzio Italia
Skipper:	Aldo Migliaccio
Designer:	Giorgetti & Magrini
Builder:	Baglietto Shipyard
Materials:	Aluminium
Launched:	1986
Length o/a:	19.55 metres
Length w/l:	13.60 metres
Beam:	3.85 metres
Displacement:	27,500 kilos
Rating:	12 Metre class
Sails by:	North
Sail area:	210 sq.metres

The success of the first Italian challenge for the America's Cup led that country's senior club, the Yacht Club Italiano, to consider mounting another challenge parallel to that from Costa Smeralda. Its first move was to purchase *Victory '83*, and the second was to hire Ian Howlett as a design consultant.

The challenge was one with enormous style and, since one of the major sponsors was the House of Gucci, that was hardly surprising. The crew were certainly the best dressed for the campaign, and at times they showed sailing talent to match their outfits.

Italia was nominally designed by Giorgetti and Magrini, but the influence of Howlett was undoubtedly there. During the 12-Metre World Championship she did display a propensity to bury her bow when going downwind and wash men off her foredeck as they were folding the headsail away! Had she been as fully developed as *White Crusader*, she might easily have made the final four after the three round-robins of challenger selection trials. She will still provide a good base for the club's next challenge.

Local Hero III

'Head for the big black cloud and find the wind' has been the dictum of many a sailing coach over the years. There are, of course, exceptions to every rule and this day in Cowes Week of 1985 was one of them — in a tactical sense, at least. There was wind a'plenty under the black cloud, but not too much to use effectively. The Solent has that knack of turning sound theory into temporary total chaos. Perhaps that is one of the reasons, the perfidious ones, why yachtsmen return to this aquatic playground and, like children there, fall down and graze their knees.

Cowes Week, by virtue of its place in the social calendar, should be a regatta of balmy breezes, a time when gentlemen, and their ladies, may enjoy a traditional British summer. Fine Cowes Weeks now regularly appear to have given way to weeks of wind and rain; or are those the ones which are all too indelibly printed on the memory?

Philippe Briand certainly did not test his design to be sailed at this angle of heel, nor would have he expected it to make the leeway that *Local Hero III*'s wake indicates that she has. The broach is complete for the One-Tonner which Geoff Howison built at High Tech Marine and which he chartered to John Ewart for the season to campaign for Britain's team in the Admiral's Cup.

It was a season of mixed results for *Local Hero III*, one in which she showed that she had the potential but in which she never fully realized it, despite some high-powered 'help' on board. It was as though she was condemned to be the bridesmaid or, more likely, that she was one of those boats for whom the luck never runs. Suffice it to say that Howison put her into the building shed for the winter to make minor modifications, repainted her in a totally new livery and renamed her *Local Hero IV*. Even that did not have the desired effect — at least, not immediately — but it may.

Name of yacht:–	LOCAL HERO III
Registered:	United Kingdom 1985
Owner:	J. Howison/High Tech Marine
Skipper:	J. Howison
Designer:	P. Briand
Builder:	High Tech Marine
Materials:	S – Glass/Kevlar/Carbon/Foam
Launched:	1985
Length o/a:	12.12 metres
Length w/l:	9.90 metres
Beam:	3.45 metres
Draft:	2.23 metres
Displacement:	5,948 kilos
Rating:	30.5 feet IOR
Sails by:	Sobstad/North
Sail area:	95 sq.metres

Coyote

Name of yacht:—	COYOTE
Registered:	France 1985
Owner:	Coyacht
Skipper:	B. Troublé
Designer:	Berret/Fauroux
Builder:	Bénéteau
Materials:	Kevlar/Carbon/Foam
Launched:	1985
Length o/a:	11.99 metres
Beam:	3.67 metres
Draft:	2.20 metres
Displacement:	5,444 kilos
Rating:	30.5 feet IOR
Sails by:	Sobstad
Sail area:	80.45 sq.metres

With her predecessor, Bruno Troublé laid waste the trophies in Cowes Week in 1984. The former America's Cup skipper and Olympic sailor found the One Ton size perfect for his foray into offshore racing. *Coyote* was constructed, as part of a short production series, by Bénéteau. She and *Phoenix* were built side by side, as part of an arrangement made by Lloyd Bankson with Troublé and Bénéteau, and the choice of who had which one was decided on the toss of a coin. The boats were complete, right down to an inventory of sails by Sobstad.

One-Tonners dominated the scene at both the 1983 and 1985 Admiral's Cup; in the latter, *Coyote* represented France and here she is doing what these relatively light displacement boats do best, spinnaker reaching in a brisk breeze on the flat water of Christchurch Bay. Interestingly, Bruno has opted to keep the number three genoa flying, using it as a staysail.

When *Coyote* went to the Sardinia Cup, as one of the French team, she was the centre of a minor storm with a pedantic International Jury and a humane Race Committee. It was the latter's insistence on reinstating *Coyote*, after the Jury had eliminated her from all races for failing to produce the final page of her rating certificate in time, which must have rankled with the sea lawyers.

Troublé was five minutes late in delivering the final page, but the Jury had had a telex from the Fédération Français à Voile a fortnight earlier which had confirmed that the certificate was in order and which gave all the relevant details as listed on the certificate. A telex is considered a legally binding document of proof internationally and, knowing the vagaries of the Italian postal system, should have been more than satisfactory for the Jury, but that body was determined to work strictly to the letter of the Notice of Race. The Race Committee of the Yacht Club Costa Smeralda acted in the interests of the sport and reinstated *Coyote*, but it was a close thing for Troublé.

Di Hard

When a team from Papua New Guinea was announced for the Admiral's Cup it occasioned some surprise in Cowes, but it was no joke. The emergent ocean-racing nation provided a more than good account of itself. That was hardly surprising, as most were expatriate Australians. It was generally reckoned that this was Australia's second team, although the performance of the Two-Tonner *Di Hard* was anything but second-rate.

This was the day of the first inshore race of the 1983 Champagne Mumm Admiral's Cup to be held outside the confines of the Solent. For many years the visitors had wailed that the British teams had had such an advantage racing on tricky waters they knew well that it was unfair to the foreign teams. They also argued that the Solent was no true test of sailing, and that what was needed were Olympic-style courses in relatively tide-free waters. In 1983 they got what they had been asking for with one race, an event which was repeated two years later. By 1987, two of the three inshore races were held over Olympic triangle-style courses in Christchurch Bay.

The first of them was unforgettable. The black storm-clouds filled in from the west and the wind shifted everywhere at all sorts of strengths. It became a test of the crews far different from that which they had expected and it also became a photographer's heyday with unusually stark contrasts for the camera.

Name of yacht:–	DI HARD
Registered:	Papua New Guinea 1983
Owner:	T. Woodward
Designer:	G. Frers
Builder:	McConaghy
Materials:	Kevlar/Carbon
Launched:	1983
Length o/a:	12.54 metres
Beam:	3.74 metres
Draft:	2.27 metres
Displacement:	6,895 kilos
Rating:	31.8 feet IOR
Sails by:	Sobstad

Diva G

Name of yacht:–	DIVA G
Registered:	Germany 1985
Owner:	Westphal-Langloh/Diekell
Skipper:	B. Beilken
Designer:	Judel/Vrolijk
Builder:	D & M/Y.W. Wedel
Materials:	Kevlar/Carbon/Foam
Launched:	1985
Length o/a:	13.27 metres
Beam:	4.19 metres
Draft:	2.38 metres
Displacement:	7,769 kilos
Rating:	33.6 feet IOR

The threatened introduction of a minimum aggregate rating limit for an Admiral's Cup team has put an end to the team of three 30-ft raters, the boats which have dominated the results in the past. It has therefore introduced a new essential size of boat to go with two One-Tonners to complete the new aggregate of rating; the 44-footer, a popular size in the past. With the aggregate raised to 95 ft for 1987 the 'big' boat of the team has been a fraction bigger with an optimum rating of 34.2 ft IOR, in order to carry an extra man in the crew.

The Hanseatic design team of Friedrich Judel and Rolf Vrolijk pre-empted the change somewhat by combining their talents to produce *Diva G* for her German owners, Peter Westphal-Langloh and Freddy Diekell, and she was built by the Yachtwerf Wedel of Kevlar and glass on a foam sandwich core. What was more significant was that she was a forerunner in the fractional rig for boats of this size, the introduction of Kevlar/Mylar laminated sailcloth and improved spar technology making this possible.

Diva G was one of a winning team and, while she did not quite match the results of her smaller team-mates during the 1985 Admiral's Cup, she did have more than her fair share of success. Much of that was due to the way in which she was handled; her crew-work was near-immaculate. She was skippered by Berend Beilken, who has been in almost every German Admiral's Cup team since 1973, and over his shoulder came instructions from the tall figure of Eric von Krausse, the navigator and tactician.

Golden Apple of the Sun

Name of yacht:–	
GOLDEN APPLE OF THE SUN	
Registered:	Ireland 1979
Owner:	H. Coveney
Skipper:	H. Cudmore
Designer:	R. Holland
Builder:	Souter
Materials:	Wood (cold moulded)
Launched:	1979
Length o/a:	13.32 metres
Beam:	3.96 metres
Draft:	2.34 metres
Displacement:	8,642 kilos
Rating:	33.1 feet IOR
Sails by:	McWilliams
Sail area:	101 sq.metres

The name is taken from the W.B. Yeats poem *Song of Wandering Aengus. Golden Apple of the Sun* was one of a pair of 44-footers, the other being *Silver Apple of the Moon*. They were built in cold-moulded wood by Souters at Cowes for the 1979 Irish Admiral's Cup trials. *Golden Apple*, with designer Ron Holland on board together with skipper Harold Cudmore, made it into the team, while *Silver Apple* was chartered to Switzerland.

She is seen here at the start of the ill-fated Fastnet, beating out of the Solent under leaden skies; bad enough, but worse was to follow. During the storm, on her way back from the Rock, *Golden Apple of the Sun* suffered, as did many others, from a broken rudder. While the crew were making plans to fit an emergency rudder a rescue helicopter flew overhead. The crew were offered a pluck to safety and, with a worsening weather forecast (one which did not materialize), the decision was made to abandon the boat and to collect it the next day. A notice was left on the main hatch: 'Gone to Lunch'!

104

Nirvana

There was a threat that the maxi-boat circuit would be dominated by covered-in day racers, or at least boats which tended to resemble them. Too much emphasis was being paid to designing and building boats which would win races, while little thought was being given to those who sometimes had to live below; hulls were great cathedral-like caverns with a huge engine in the middle (for rating purposes) and very little else. Marvin Green was determined that his maxi should not be another of those.

On the other hand, *Nirvana* had to be capable of winning races, and so some of her interior was made removable and replaced when the boat was being cruised. The job of designing such a boat fell to David Pedrick, and the construction (in aluminium, somewhat naturally) to Palmer Johnson of Sturgeon Bay, Wisconsin. The result was an unqualified success, right from her launching in April, 1982.

The 81-footer has been optimized to a 70 ft IOR rating and can sail to it. Here she is bashing her way to windward just after the start of the Channel Race in 1985 and when she returned it was with a Class A corrected time victory and the race record time destroyed. It is, however, only one of the race records which *Nirvana* holds. Soon after she was launched she broke the record for the Newport—Bermuda Race, and then added more to it; the Gozo Race in Malta, Block Island Race and the China Sea Race from Hong Kong to Manila in 1984, after a battle with *Condor* all the way.

This followed a similar battle with the same boat in the 1983 Sydney—Hobart Race which concluded with *Nirvana* finishing first but being disqualified on protest after a luffing incident four miles from the finish. But one triumph that could not be taken away was her 1985 performance in the Fastnet when she beat *Atlantic Privateer* home by 23 seconds to set yet another course record.

Name of yacht:–	NIRVANA
Registered:	United States of America 1985
Owner:	M. Green Jnr.
Designer:	D. Pedrick
Builder:	Palmer Johnson
Materials:	Aluminium
Launched:	1982
Length o/a:	24.69 metres (81ft)
Length w/l:	20.42 metres (67ft)
Beam:	5.6 metres (18ft 4in)
Draft:	3.95 metres (13ft)
Displacement:	38,483 kilos (84,778 lb)
Rating:	69.7 feet IOR
Sails by:	Hood
Sail area:	314.2 sq.metres (3,382 sq.feet)

Equity & Law

At the heart of all offshore racing is the production cruiser/racer, and in the upper echelon of these is the Baltic 55, of which *Equity & Law* is an example. It was the design, by Doug Peterson, which was chosen by Dutchman Pleun van der Lugt for his entry in the 1985—86 Whitbread Round the World Race, chosen because he had confidence in the reliability of the products of Baltic Yachts in Finland, in view of the performance of *Skopbank of Finland*, a Baltic 51, in the previous race.

Pleun interested the insurance company Equity & Law of Holland in backing his project, following the second overall success of his countryman Conny van Rietschoten in the race. The two became acquainted when van der Lugt was sailing single-handed non-stop around the world in his 35-ft De Zeeuwse at the same time that the 1981-82 Whitbread was in progress, and they used to talk to each other over the radio whenever they were in close enough contact.

When they met after their circumnavigations, van Rietschoten encouraged van der Lugt into entering the Whitbread race, an event he had discussed many times with Chay Blyth when they raced the 65-ft trimaran *Lonsdale Cars* (ex-*Brittany Ferries GB*) in the Plymouth—Vilamoura—Plymouth race. It may have been due to this experience that his criteria for his crew included 'men with excellent sailing qualifications, unconditional dedication and a high degree of tolerance'. They were the criteria of a serviceman and Pleun had been in the Royal Dutch Air Force.

They were almost enough to win him Class D in the race. Only a spreader failure (which sent him back into port halfway through the first leg) spoiled his chances. *Equity & Law* had a tremendous tussle with *Rucanor Tri Star* for the other three legs, winning her class on two occasions and being second overall to the eventual race winner, *L'Esprit d'Equipe*, on the leg around Cape Horn, from Auckland to Punta del Este.

Name of yacht:—	EQUITY & LAW
Registered:	Holland 1985
Skipper:	P. van der Lugt
Designer:	D. Peterson
Builder:	Baltic Yachts
Materials:	GRP/Balsa
Launched:	1984
Length o/a:	16.7 metres
Length w/l:	14.4 metres
Beam:	4.7 metres
Draft:	3.0 metres
Displacement:	16,219 kilos
Rating:	44.4 feet IOR
Sail area:	163.2 sq.metres

French Kiss

Name of yacht:–	FRENCH KISS
Registered:	France 1986
Owner:	S.Crasnianski/Kis France
Skipper:	M.Pajot
Designer:	P. Briand
Builder:	Alubat
Materials:	Aluminium
Launched:	1985
Length o/a:	20.50 metres
Length w/l:	14.00 metres
Draft:	2.8 metres
Displacement:	26,000 kilos
Rating:	12 Metre class
Sails by:	Voile Systeme/Tasker/Cheret
Sail area:	240 sq.metres

Generally considered one of the most elegant of the modern 12-Metres, until the savage slicing of 80 cm from her stern immediately prior to the semi-finals of the challenger selection trials for the 1987 America's Cup, *French Kiss* was the first 12-Metre boat designed by Philippe Briand, whose level rating IOR boats had become highly regarded. She was unique among her competitors in Fremantle in not having been subjected to model tank testing, Briand relying instead entirely on computer analysis.

The project was the brainchild of skipper Marc Pajot, who renounced his multihull offshore racing for three years to become involved with the America's Cup. The finance came from the Kis 'fast everything' empire of Serge Crasnianski and that brought with it the first serious objection. The Royal Perth Yacht Club refused to allow her to race under that name, which it believed contravened the IYRU Rule 26. Covering the name, she raced under her sail number, F 7, in the practice races of the World Championship but for the event itself she reverted to her name when the International Jury cleared its use, saying 'French Kiss' was a phrase known and used prior to its appearance as the name of the yacht, and that with a second 's' it did not represent the company which had financed the boat.

That was the first of the shocks for which *French Kiss* was responsible. The next came when she won two of the championship races and everyone began to take a new view of the French challenge. She continued in that manner during the early races for the Louis Vuitton Cup — the prize for the winner of the challenger selection trials for the America's Cup — reaching the semi-finals, where she went down in four straight races to *New Zealand 7*.

Her other triumph was in the graphics which she brought with her. The tee-shirts and other Cup ephemera with her name on them were easily the most sought after in Fremantle; in all things, *French Kiss* had style.

Gloria

The combination of the grace of the past with the technology of the future has created in *Gloria* one of the truly great ocean thoroughbreds. Here is a majestic boat which at first glance might be taken for one built early in the century — but she was launched in March 1986.

Gloria was designed by Pieter Beeldsnijder (from the cheese town of Edam) and built in Holland of steel, stainless where it was considered necessary to combat wear and tear, to the highest possible standards regardless of cost — and it shows. Since she was built with world cruising in mind, it was considered essential to have the most durable construction possible.

The superstructures are all in aluminium, to reduce unnecessary weight, while throughout her interior *Gloria* is panelled in mahogany. It does not stop there — the six bathrooms have individual marble work and there are two open fireplaces in the saloons. *Gloria* also has a library, exquisite marine paintings and a piano. Comfort for the owner and his guests was one of the prime considerations in the concept of this 166-ton staysail schooner.

Ease of handling of the rig was another. Both masts are of the 'stow-away' principle with sails furling inside them. All the sails are roller furling and the furlers are driven by hydraulic motors under a Lewmar Commander which also controls the major winches. It is push-button sailing, and if the wind dies away there is a 400 hp Caterpillar diesel to push this 128-footer along, together with a special four-bladed, variable-pitch propellor. The only drawback, and there has to be a serpent in this Eden, is that she draws over 13 feet.

Name of yacht:–	GLORIA
Registered:	United Kingdom 1986
Owner:	Ragne Shipping
Designer:	P. Beeldsnijder
Builder:	Jongert/Lowland Yachts
Materials:	Steel
Launched:	1986
Length o/a:	38.40 metres
Length w/l:	23.90 metres
Beam:	6.90 metres
Draft:	4.02 metres
Sails by:	Hood
Sail area:	640 sq.metres

Flyer I

Name of yacht:–	FLYER I
Registered:	Holland 1977
Owner:	C. van Reitschoten
Skipper:	C. van Reitschoten
Designer:	Sparkman & Stephens
Builder:	Huisman
Materials:	Aluminium
Launched:	1977
Length o/a:	19.87 metres
Length w/l:	15.21 metres
Beam:	5.00 metres
Draft:	3.05 metres
Displacement:	25,084 kilos
Rating:	48.4 feet IOR
Sails by:	Hood
Sail area:	169.73 sq.metres

When Conny van Rietschoten set out to compete in the Whitbread Round the Word Race in 1977 he went to the designers of the boat which had won the previous race and gave them carte blanche to provide him with a boat which would win. Sparkman & Stephens answered with the 65-ft ketch *Flyer*, a development of the Swan 65 design *Sayula II* which had won the original race. She was built, in aluminium alloy, by Wolter Huisman.

The Madison Avenue firm of naval architects provided a relatively heavy-displacement boat with a ketch rig because of the large amount of windward sailing and the ease with which sail reductions could be made. It was almost too easy, but for three legs of the race there was some close racing with a sloop-rigged Swan 65, *King's Legend*, although wrong choice of course on the Cape Horn leg put her out of the running. *Flyer* won the race by two and a half days on corrected time.

Flyer II

Van Rietschoten's aim in the third Whitbread Race was to be first into every port and for that he went to German Frers for a maxi-rater. The 77-footer was again built by Wolter Huisman in aluminium alloy, and rated 67.7 ft IOR. Her owner campaigned her fully on both sides of the Atlantic before she lined up at Portsmouth in September 1981, finding many of the minor problems and correcting them before the main event.

Flyer II proved to be the ideal boat for her intended purpose; she was fast and her crew delighted in pushing her close to the limit. Conny did that to himself

too and suffered a minor heart attack on the second leg, deep in the Southern Ocean. He received medical advice from the doctor on the nearest boat, the rival *Ceramco New Zealand*, while he demanded that the crew should not slow upon his account.

They did not, and when van Rietschoten was cleared by doctors in Auckland he decided to continue with the race and achieved his aim. But even greater rewards were to be his when *Charles Heidsieck III* went the wrong way at the North Atlantic High and lost so much time that the handicap prize went to *Flyer II* as well.

Name of yacht:–	FLYER II
Registered:	Holland 1981
Owner:	C. van Reitschoten
Skipper:	C. van Reitschoten
Designer:	G. Frers
Builder:	Huisman
Materials:	Aluminium
Launched:	1980
Length o/a:	23.16 metres
Length w/l:	19.81 metres
Beam:	5.49 metres
Draft:	3.57 metres
Displacement:	30,386 kilos
Rating:	67.7 feet IOR
Sails by:	Hood

Great Britain II

Name of yacht:	GREAT BRITAIN II
Registered:	United Kingdom 1977
Owner:	Chay Blyth
Designer:	A. Gurney
Builder:	Bayside Marine
Materials:	Airex-cored GRP
Launched:	1973
Length o/a:	23.64 metres
Length w/l:	20.18 metres
Beam:	5.32 metres
Draft:	2.83 metres
Displacement:	38,129 kilos
Rating:	69.2 feet IOR
Sail area:	268 sq.metres

There can never have been a yacht which has raced more miles — and included in that would be *Britannia* — than *Great Britain II* in one or other of her guises. Five times she has raced around the world for a total of 130,000 miles and in her other races and charter work she will have doubled that distance.

Great Britain II was built in foam sandwich by Bayside Marine at Sandwich for Chay Blyth and his crew from the Parachute Regiment for the first Whitbread Round the World Race of 1973–74. She had to be all British, as she was sponsored by Jack Hayward and his patriotic intensity forbade foreign effort. Nevertheless, it was an expatriate, Alan Gurney, who drew her lines, a development from *Windward Passage*.

Blyth and his crew had a mixed race. It took them some time to understand the way the boat should be sailed and then one man was lost overboard in the Southern Ocean; but they did establish the fastest elapsed time, 144 days 10 hours. That record disappeared when the boat, with an all-services crew, won the Financial Times Clipper Race, with a single stop in Sydney, in a little over 134 days.

In 1977, when part of Blyth's charter fleet, *Great Britain II* was again on the starting line for the Whitbread, but this time with Rob James as skipper and a fare-paying crew. James took the first leg to get them into shape, but from there on he was determined to beat Blyth's time — and he did, by ten days.

Four years later, under the ownership of Cecilia Unger, the boat was back again, rerigged as a sloop and again skippered by Blyth. She had been renamed *United Friendly*, and just managed to beat her original time in what was generally regarded as a slow race. Bob Salmon took her in the fourth Whitbread of 1985–86, as *Norsk Data GB*, and looked set to beat her all-time record when the wind went sour on the final leg and she coasted in in 138 days. On wonders whether she will be there in 1989, or if indeed they will start the Whitbread without her.

High Roler

High Roler was built for Bill Power by Eric Goetz of a composite carbon fibre/S glass laminate and launched in time for the 1985 SORC. A 43-footer, rating 33.5, *High Roler* was soon showing near the front of her division. The Californian design team of Nelson/Marek chose a masthead rig for her and she made selection to the US Admiral's Cup team from the trials held in Newport, Rhode Island. In those trials the selectors had pointed out that only those boats rating less than 33.5 ft IOR would be considered for the team; *High Roler* just made it inside the upper limit, for earlier she had rated 33.6 ft.

In Cowes *High Roler* was the top-scoring boat in the US team. In the second inshore race, Power adopted an old Solent adage, perhaps even unwittingly, in a light northerly breeze — that you go north when the wind is from the north. Those who went the other way that day were part of history. That and another break as the fleet headed for Gaff buoy were to make the day for Power. *High Roler* went on to win the 30-miler by just under two minutes to take home the extremely elegant Corum Trophy.

In the third inshore race of that series, *High Roler* was third behind *Phoenix* and *Caiman*, while in the Fastnet she was first of the 'bigger' boats among the Admiral's Cuppers, at eighth behind seven One-Tonners.

Bill Power has continued to race the boat with some élan, firstly by ensuring that she was back in San Francisco to compete in the Big Boat Series, less than a month after the Fastnet, and taking top prize in her division. In the 1986 SORC, *High Roler* won class C and was fifth overall.

Name of yacht:–	HIGH ROLER
Registered:	United States of America 1985
Owner:	W. Power
Skipper:	W. Power
Designer:	Nelson/Marek Inc
Builder:	E. Goetz
Materials:	Carbon/S-Glass
Launched:	1985
Length o/a:	13.03 metres (42ft 9in)
Length w/l:	10.36 metres (34ft)
Beam:	4.06 metres (13ft 4in)
Draft:	2.45 metres (8ft)
Displacement:	8,407 kilos (18,521 lb)
Rating:	33.5 feet IOR
Sails by:	North
Sail area:	99.7 sq.metres (1,073 sq.feet)

Philips Innovator

With the electronics giant Philips (whose chairman Gerry Jeelof is an ocean-racing sailor) behind him, Dirk Nauta was able to prepare a formidable entry for the fourth Whitbread race of 1985/86. It was to be an all-Dutch affair, so Rolf Vrolijk was commissioned to design a boat aimed at winning the handicap prize.

Any review of past races would show that a boat of between 60 ft and 65 ft overall would have the best chance; *Sayula II* and the first *Flyer* were both 65-footers and *Charles Heidsieck III*, which was leading the third race until she ran out of wind, was 66 ft. Nauta chose a slightly shorter overall boat than those, at 63 ft, but with a 56-ft waterline. The boat has powerful lines, capable of carrying plenty of sail downwind in a strong breeze.

She was not able to show that potential when she went to the SORC as part of her training prior to the Round the World Race, Nauta finding out that the boat was somewhat unstable. On her return to Holland, and after consultations with Vrolijk, a heavier keel was fitted and a new, lighter mast stepped. The difference was marked.

On the first leg, to Cape Town, *Philips Innovator* was second on corrected time, to *L'Esprit d'Equipe*. The next leg saw her take the leg prize and the overall lead; the two-sail reaching in the Southern Ocean had suited her well. On the Cape Horn leg she was only fourth and lost her lead while on the final leg to Portsmouth. Nauta again claimed second on corrected time to clinch second place overall. 'Next time,' he said, as though there was never any doubt, 'it will be a maxi.'

Name of yacht:–	PHILIPS INNOVATOR
Registered:	Holland 1985
Owner:	D. Nauta
Skipper:	D. Nauta
Designer:	R.Vrolijk
Builder:	Aluboot
Materials:	Aluminium
Launched:	1984
Length o/a:	19.20 metres
Beam:	5.12 metres
Draft:	3.33 metres
Displacement:	22,859 kilos
Rating:	52.2 feet IOR
Sails by:	Hood
Sail area:	198 sq.metres

Hitchhiker II

Name of yacht:	HITCHHIKER II
Registered:	Australia 1985
Owner:	P. Briggs
Skipper:	N. Robins
Designer:	G. Frers
Builder:	M. Baker
Materials:	Carbon/Divinycell
Launched:	1985
Length o/a:	12.19 metres
Beam:	3.60 metres
Draft:	2.12 metres
Displacement:	5,843 kilos
Rating:	30.4 feet IOR
Sail area:	81.1 sq.metres

'I was more than happy with what German Frers had produced for me last time, so I thought that I would give him a whirl again,' said Peter Briggs when asked about his new boat before it was built. 'It will be very different from any boat he has ever done before,' he added with a grin.

Then came the revelations. It was to be a fractionally rigged One-Tonner, and German had forsaken his natural conservatism to go for light displacement. The owner admitted that it would look like a boat from one of the French designers, but claimed that it would have that something extra, that magic which is Frers, and that it would be a more than adequate replacement for the Two Ton World Champion which Briggs had campaigned before.

Mike Baker built *Hitchhiker II* very carefully in Perth from carbon-fibre and S glass with a Divinycell foam core but her launch almost coincided with the Australian Admiral's Cup trials and she failed to make the team even with Noel Robins as skipper and a crew of hot-shots. Instead she raced for Papua New Guinea, collecting the requisite number of expatriate Australians to do so.

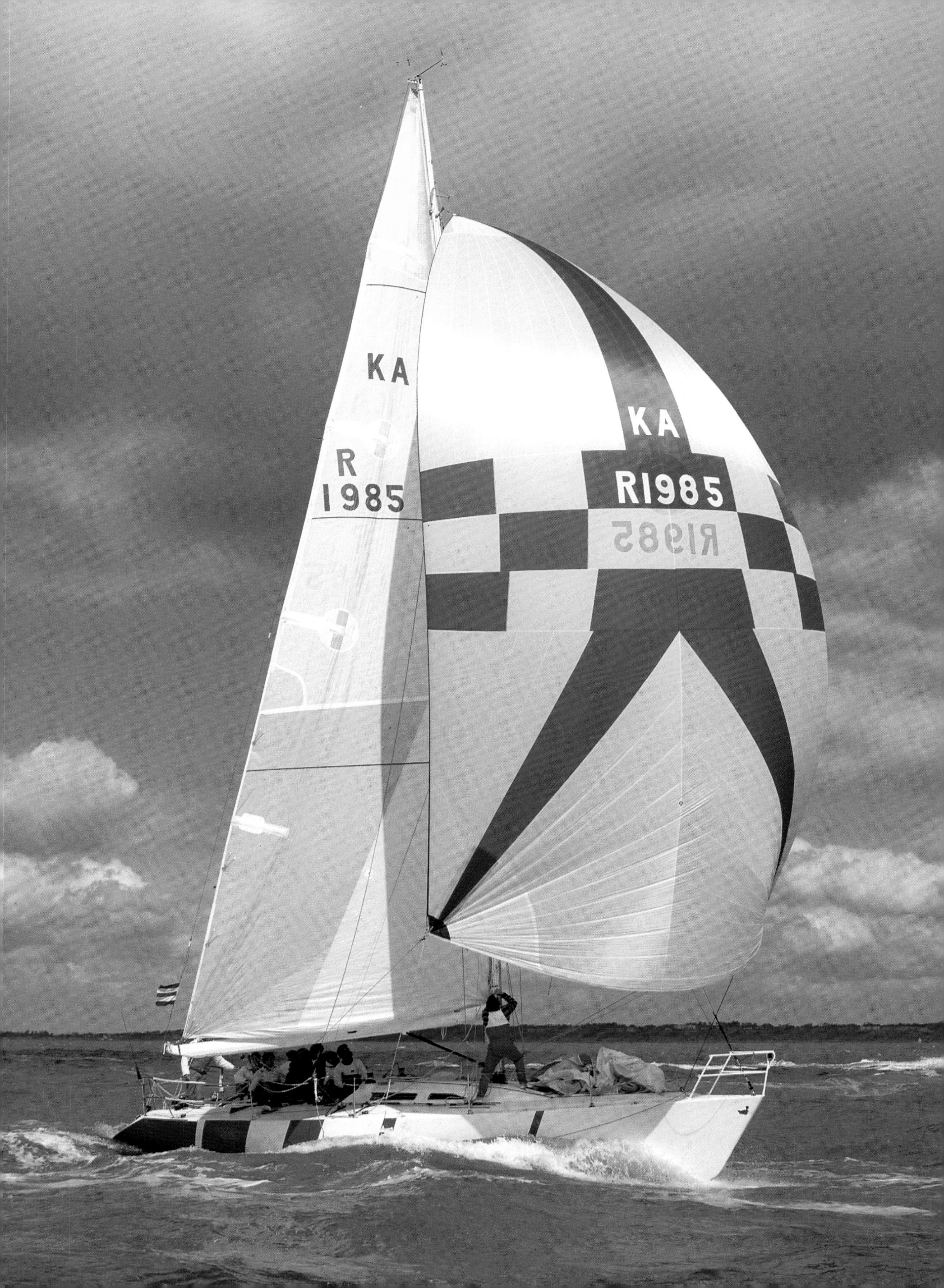
KA
R
1985
KA
R1985

Imp

Imp made every previous offshore racer obsolete from the minute she was launched. Dave Allen, her Californian owner, encouraged Ron Holland to go full out to produce a fast boat through his innovative line drawings and also through some radical technology in her building. Holland was radical and was constantly under pressure from Allen to go to the limits. The two had sailed together on the Gary Mull *Improbable*, and over the years had discussed what was necessary to make a boat fast. They had carefully eliminated all the obstacles.

Holland was therefore able to explore every pathway in his search for speed. The concept of *Imp* was for him not to have to worry greatly over the eventual IOR rating but to concentrate on a high-speed hull form with greater than usual stability and a powerful stern section, away from the then-popular 'pintails' which he and Peterson had been producing, to give the boat a good performance when reaching in fresh winds. In doing so he produced a boat which would race with the Two-Tonners while rating more than a foot less.

Holland worked with his brother-in-law, Gary Carlin, who ran the Kiwi Yachts yard, on the construction of *Imp* and, from the ideas which they had tried on a Quarter-Tonner, *Business Machine*, Holland designed his first yacht with a full box-sectioned 'H' frame to take the loads of the rig and keel. It was built into the hull and tied together with a space frame which allowed the hull skin to be very light. The skin was glass-fibre with a balsa core and some carbon-fibre reinforcement.

Imp won the SORC with an outstanding performance and was part of the US Admiral's Cup team in 1977. That year she was top-scoring individual boat, winning the third inshore race and the Fastnet. She was back in the team two years later and although she did not quite repeat that performance she was top scorer in her team, third overall, and fifth in the storm-tossed Fastnet.

Name of yacht:–	IMP
Registered:	United States of America 1979
Owner:	D. Allen
Skipper:	D. Allen
Designer:	R. Holland
Builder:	Kiwi Yachts
Materials:	GRP/Balsa
Launched:	1977
Length o/a:	12.03 metres (39ft 6in)
Beam:	3.78 metres (12ft 5in)
Draft:	2.09 metres (6ft 10in)
Displacement:	6,350 kilos (13,989 lb)
Rating:	30.9 feet IOR

Pinta, Gitana VII and Marloo II

Two-Tonners all, at a gybe mark off Porto Cervo during the 1980 Sardinia Cup. Here the wakes begin to tell the story, but only part of it. Each one of these three went high on the first of the two reaches and ended by having to run off square for the mark. Doubtless they were forced high, first by *Marloo II* going for the wind of *Gitana VII* and then by the two of them, in turn, going for the wind of *Pinta*.

In return *Pinta* was keen to protect her inside overlap going into the mark, and may have tried to pull away towards the mark earlier than the other two. This manoeuvre she has managed to complete successfully, and almost finished her gybe without giving away too much at the buoy. The wind-driven surface current that exists off the Sardinian coast has, however, carried her half a boat's length to leeward of the mark, but she is in far better shape than the other two.

Marloo II has gybed early, hoping that she can cross *Gitana VII's* stern when she gybes, but has put herself in a very dangerous position, on port tack. She must keep clear of the French boat, and it would seem that *Gitana VII* is not far enough ahead to allow *Marloo II's* helmsman the chance to slip across his stern.

Much depends on exactly what is the course to the next mark and, judging by the collapse of her spinnaker, *Pinta* is either too high for it or it will be very shy. The likelihood is, however, that all three will sail the next leg in line astern, each locked into the other's stern wave and without any extra speed to break clear.

Pinta

Willi Illbruck may have felt out in the cold for some time, but not when he commissioned Minnefords to build him this Peterson design, a development of *Eclipse*, the 1979 top points-scorer in the Admiral's Cup. She was a relatively small boat to be built in aluminium alloy, but it did enable her owner to carry out extensive alterations to her after her first season.

Before the 1981 Admiral's Cup Illbruck consulted with the Judel/Vrolijk team on the possibilities of improving his boat. As a result of their research (similar to that which Hans-Otto Schumann used to carry out with his Sparkman & Stephens designs), the bow was reshaped and the forward waterline extended by 17 cm, the after girth station moved forward by 10cm. *Pinta* was also given a new keel; she was hardly a Peterson boat any more but a Judel/Vrolijk one, and that was a pointer to the future of the top-class German offshore racers, certainly for new boats for Illbruck.

Pinta is seen here bashing her way to windward shortly after the start of an offshore race of the 1980 Sardinia Cup. The wind is fresh enough for her to set a number five jib and tuck all but one of the available reefs into her mainsail. She would benefit from the crew getting to the weather rail as she pounds into the short Mediterranean seas along the gaunt, dramatic coastline where the once volcanic hills form the Costa Smeralda.

Twenty-four hours later, having twice crossed the two-faced waters of the Straits of Bonifacio, the crew were back in Porto Cervo, slaking their thirsts in the Clipper Bar. They agreed that if they had to face that type of weather there were few places they would rather do it, and certainly not in their home waters of the Baltic.

Name of yacht:—	PINTA
Registered:	Germany 1980
Owner:	W. Illbruck
Designer:	D. Peterson
Builder:	Minneford
Materials:	Aluminium
Launched:	1980
Length o/a:	12.07 metres
Displacement:	6,766 kilos
Rating:	30.9 feet IOR

I-Punkt

Name of yacht:	I-PUNKT
Registered:	Germany 1985
Owner:	T. Friese
Skipper:	T. Friese
Designer:	Judel/Vrolijk
Builder:	Schutz/Y.W.Wedel
Materials:	Kevlar/Carbon/Honeycomb
Launched:	1985
Length o/a:	12.87 metres
Beam:	3.97 metres
Draft:	2.26 metres
Displacement:	7,016 kilos
Rating:	32.0 feet IOR
Sails by:	North/Hood
Sail area:	93.27 sq.metres

The Solent is a place of many moods; one day it can be nature's playground for yachtsmen, the next it can be positively foul. In between it provides a broad spectrum of climatic conditions and tidal variations, which is very probably the reason why so many persist in sailing these waters. Cowes Week almost invariably sees several different faces of the Solent; gone, it seems, are the balmy days with strawberries and cream for tea on the Squadron lawn which filled the columns of 'Bookstall' Smith and his son Anthony, who wrote *Sacred Cowes*.

One wonders, would King George V have raced *Britannia* on a day like this when the One-Tonners scurry eastward before a squall that promises more than a shower of rain to come? If he had, the 'company' would have gone below decks and allowed Sir Philip Hunloke to steer the boat to another victory — and doubtless a Beken would have been there to record it for posterity.

And would the King have approved of today's 'disposable' boats, ones which have a short racing career? Thomas Friese, of Japanese/German extraction, raced *I-Punkt* for Austria after failing to qualify for the 1985 German Admiral's Cup team. His failure to do so was hardly surprising; *I-Punkt* was built with a Kevlar/carbon-fibre sandwich over a pre-preg honeycomb core in just 28 days by Udo Schütz and the Yachtwerf Wedel and launched on the eve of the trials. It was a process far removed from the building of *Britannia* and only possible because she was a clone of the Judel/Vrolijk 42-footers, *Pinta* and *Container*, for which the building patterns existed.

Jade

Name of yacht:–	JADE
Registered:	United Kingdom 1985
Owner:	L. & D. Wooddell
Skipper:	L. Wooddell
Designer:	R. Humphreys
Builder:	Thompson/Feloy
Materials:	Kevlar/Carbon/Foam
Launched:	1985
Length o/a:	12.04 metres
Beam:	3.44 metres
Draft:	2.08 metres
Displacement:	5,470 kilos
Rating:	30.5 feet IOR
Sails by:	Banks/North
Sail area:	77.86 sq.metres

Jade came as a vote of confidence in designer Rob Humphreys by owners Larry and Debbie Wooddell. Rob had designed their previous One-Tonner (also *Jade*) which just failed to be selected for the Admiral's Cup in 1983, although many thought that she should have been. She was one of the three which went Down Under for the Southern Cross Cup and the Wooddells were keen to replace her with an all-out racing boat along the parameters which the French had suggested with some force.

From the earliest design stage, David Howlett became involved as project manager, and he supervised the building of this high-tech composite plastics yacht by the Thompson/Feloy partnership. The result was a boat which was fast from the very beginning, set up well by Howlett and helped in her tuning by the thoroughness of Debbie Wooddell's data-keeping. The addition of Rodney Pattisson to steer her added an extra edge to her performance.

Throughout the British Cup trials there never seemed any doubt that *Jade* would be top boat, and her selection was automatic for both the big event and, equally important, the One Ton Cup. In Poole Bay the *Jade* team were almost out of the competition when she was hit and badly holed, but in typical fashion Wooddell and Howlett saw to it that the repairs were made to the hole in the hull overnight, and they were racing the next day. Meanwhile they sought redress from the International Jury by claiming average points from the race in which they suffered the damage.

The incident may have been the inspiration for the performance which brought the One Ton Cup to England for the first time since 1974. That trophy under her belt, *Jade* went into the Admiral's Cup as the boat to beat, and she may have suffered from some close covering from boats from other nations. She was not able to add a share of the Admiral's Cup to her One Ton Cup, particularly when she lost her mast in the Fastnet.

Jennie M

Designed by German Frers and built in Lymington by Green Marine, the 44-ft *Jennie M* was one of the clutch of Admiral's Cup contenders of 1985. She did not make the team, despite having Owen Parker as sailing master, a role he undertook successfully aboard a succession of *Morning Clouds*, but she was always one of the front runners.

Life for an offshore racer is not all Cups and trials, particularly those which are based in the Solent — there is more to life than that. But it is there that the races may be said to constitute the basis of Britain's major competitions, the Solent Points Championship and the RORC Offshore Championship, both of which *Jennie M* contested with success. Here broad reaching eastwards before a dark rain squall, Parker has decided not to drop the number four genoa, but to use it as a staysail instead.

Parker was one of the earliest advocates of holding a genoa under a spinnaker and his three-sail reaching technique was gradually adopted by many in the early 1970s. Flatter, broader-shouldered spinnakers and better staysail technology have tended to overtake the old technique but on days when the wind blows hard it is probably better to get the men off the foredeck as quickly as possible when there is only a small headsail which will not provide a great deal of interference, particularly if the leg is a short one. Solent Points races often have many short legs to test the crews, and on the more blustery of the days they know when they have been tested.

Name of yacht:—	JENNIE M
Registered:	United Kingdom 1985
Owner:	J. Meller
Designer:	G. Frers
Builder:	Green Marine
Materials:	GRP/Foam
Launched:	1985
Length o/a:	13.52 metres
Length w/l:	11.03 metres
Beam:	4.04 metres
Draft:	2.60 metres
Displacement:	8.804 kilos
Rating:	35 feet IOR
Sails by:	North/Sobstad
Sail area:	106.6 sq.metres

Moonduster

Name of yacht:–	MOONDUSTER
Registered:	Ireland 1985
Owner:	D. Doyle
Skipper:	D. Doyle
Designer:	G. Frers
Builder:	Crosshaven Boatyard
Materials:	Wood/Carbon
Launched:	1981
Length o/a:	15.61 metres
Beam:	4.43 metres
Draft:	2.70 metres
Displacement:	14,085 kilos
Rating:	39.8 feet IOR
Sails by:	McWilliams
Sail area:	142 sq.metres

The stories of Dennis Doyle's 51-ft, Frers-designed *Moonduster* are legion, as would befit 'yer man from the Royal Cork Yacht Club'. The fact that he had to buy the Crosshaven Boatyard (which was building her) is only one of them, but for two Admiral's Cups the mahogany topsides of *Moonduster* have graced the Irish team as their flagship each time. No one will forget how she went into the darkening water of the western Solent in the first race in 1983 and led the fleet home.

Nor will they forget her performance offshore, like the occasion when she chased *Midnight Sun* home to be second in the 1981 Channel Race or even her finish, without a mast, at the end of the 1983 Fastnet. That brought the comment from Dennis' wife, Mary, 'Dennis, if you want to take up powerboat racing, you should get a boat with a bigger engine!' One wonders how he felt when, here at the start of the next Fastnet Race, he faced a westerly of 40 knots and more; would he then have wished that he had taken up powerboat racing?

Sidewinder

It is not unknown for a committed East Coaster to make the effort to go to Cowes for some of the big races. Bob Watson did it with *Cervantes* in 1971, to become a member of a successful Admiral's Cup team, but the migration has lately become more permanent. John Oswald is one of the exceptions. Staunchly rooted on the River Crouch, his forays have only been essential ones.

One of his first ventures was to ask designer Hugh Welbourn for the lines of a fractionally rigged One-Tonner and then he decided that Neville Hutton should build the boat at the Sadler's Farm 'marine complex' on Pennington Marshes outside Lymington. Hutton and Welbourn decided that glass-fibre over a cedar core would provide a strong, light hull with sufficient durability to give Oswald the type of racing he would enjoy for several years; first on the grand prix circuit and then in the cut and thrust of the East Anglian Offshore Racing Association series and a few of the deep-sea and short-handed races which he loves.

Sidewinder tackled the Admiral's Cup trials in 1985, and the One Ton Cup, but her most noted success came the following year when she claimed line honours in the race from Plymouth to San Sebastian in Spain. On her return she looked into Cowes on her way back to Burnham-on-Crouch. In typical cavalier fashion, Oswald entered for the Rocking Chair Trophy and went home to relax in it. A week later he was engaged in a head-to-head scrap with *Backlash* for superiority on the Crouch at Burnham Week, that East Coast festival of sailing and socializing, and went down only narrowly.

Name of yacht:–	SIDEWINDER
Registered:	United Kingdom 1985
Owner:	J. Oswald
Skipper:	J. Oswald
Designer:	H. Welbourn
Builder:	N. Hutton
Materials:	GRP/Cedar
Launched:	1984
Length o/a:	12.13 metres
Length w/l:	10.36 metres
Beam:	3.7 metres
Draft:	2.15 metres
Displacement:	5,706 kilos
Rating:	30.5 feet IOR
Sails by:	Hood/Banks
Sail area:	80.45 sq.metres

Jubilation

Name of yacht:–	JUBILATION
Registered:	United States of America 1985
Owner:	J. James
Skipper:	G. Jobson
Designer:	G. Frers
Builder:	Goetz
Materials:	GRP/Foam
Launched:	1983
Length o/a:	16.40 metres (53ft 10in)
Length w/l:	13.44 metres (44ft 1in)
Beam:	4.73 metres (15ft 6in)
Draft:	2.92 metres (9ft 7in)
Displacement:	14,832 kilos (32,675 lb)
Rating:	43.1 feet IOR
Sails by:	North
Sail area:	133.78 sq.metres (1,440 sq.feet)

It was not long after this picture was taken that I lost all chance of appearing in any of the royal Honours Lists, since I was at the wheel of *Jubilation* that day as we ran towards one of the marks at the entrance to Southampton Water. On board for the Queen's Cup was the great-great-grandson of Queen Victoria (who had presented the trophy to the Royal Southampton Yacht Club), Prince Michael of Kent.

It is one of those courses that you are none too keen to sail; dead downwind with a capful of breeze and a building sea against the tide. In addition, you are trying to avoid any possible deviation to windward as that will certainly mean two gybes and the resultant risks are better not to contemplate. It is the true Catch 22.

Jubilation was built in high-tech composite plastics to German Frers designs, and is 54 ft overall. Jack James, her owner, had decided to campaign her in Britain for Cowes Week and the Fastnet, and early in the season skipper Gary Jobson asked me to provide some local knowledge. Just how HRH joined the crew is a long story but how he became the 'drown' Prince bears telling.

Suffice to say the buoy was almost bearing by the lee when one of the waves lifted the stern, pushing the bow off to leeward. Despite plenty of wheel-turning to correct it, *Jubilation* went into a Chinese gybe and for a moment (it seemed like a quarter of an hour) she was pinned with the rail under water. I had the feeling of being dragged through it when HRH plummeted from the high side into the water! Fortunately, he fell into the lifelines and, sportsman that he is, had the presence of mind to hang on. Needless to say, the incident cost *Jubilation* the Queen's Cup.

Justine IV

'X stands for the unknown factor,' Frank X. Woods will tell you; but there is little that was unknown about his 40-ft *Justine IV*. For a start, she was named after his daughter, as was his previous boat designed by Tony Castro, which won the One Ton Cup off Cork with five firsts in five races.

Frank Woods likes nothing better than winning, and in commissioning this boat he left very little to chance. He went again to Castro, the man who had served him well before, for a minimum rater for the 1983 Admiral's Cup and drew around him the Cork 'mafia', including Harold Cudmore as skipper. This brought the comment from Ron Holland: 'Harry's going to make Castro look good this year!' Or should it have been the other way around? It might have been from anyone but a rival designer. *Justine IV* went on to prove how good she was in the following two years when, as *Whirlwind XI*, she was twice RORC Yacht of the Year.

Killian Bushe, who has stood at the point of the boat many times for Cudmore, built *Justine IV* in a glass-fibre/foam sandwich using vinylester resin, and Johnny McWilliams made the sails. Both sailed on her with Robert Dix as helmsman. *Justine IV* won all seven of the Irish Admiral's Cup trials, the Morgan Cup, was top offshore points scorer in the Admiral's Cup and third overall individually in that event. Frank's X may be the unknown factor but it was certainly successful, whatever it was.

Name of yacht:–	JUSTINE IV
Registered:	Ireland 1983
Owner:	F. Woods
Skipper:	H. Cudmore
Designer:	A. Castro
Builder:	K. Bushe
Materials:	Kevlar/Carbon
Launched:	1983
Length o/a:	12.06 metres
Beam:	3.76 metres
Draft:	2.16 metres
Displacement:	5,717 kilos
Rating:	30.1 feet IOR
Sails by:	McWilliams
Sail area:	78 sq.metres

Lady Be

Name of yacht: –	LADY BE
Registered:	France 1983
Owner:	Chantiers Bénéteau
Skipper:	P. Blake (charter)
Designer:	G. Frers
Builder:	Bénéteau
Materials:	Kevlar/Carbon/Foam
Launched:	1983
Length o/a:	13.81 metres
Length w/l:	11.64 metres
Beam:	4.21 metres
Draft:	2.50 metres
Displacement:	9,225 kilos
Rating:	35.4 feet IOR
Sails by:	North

Neville Crichton named his 44-ft Frers design — very appropriately as things turned out — *Shockwave*. She was to cause all sorts of consternation; among Australian yachting administrators who didn't want to pick her for the Admiral's Cup because she was owned by a New Zealander, and among her competitors when she won five out of the first nine of those trials. Her performance, however, caused some slight grief in the offices of Bénéteau; they needed a boat like her in their production range, and with some modification Frers produced the 456 for the French builders.

Eric Duchemin was recruited by Bénéteau to campaign the first off the line in the French Admiral's Cup trials and just failed to gain a place, but the boat, *Lady Be*, came under the eagle eye of Peter Blake, who was looking for one to charter for the New Zealand team where she would join *Shockwave*; a somewhat bizarre circumstance.

There was none too much of the 'production' about *Lady Be*, with her Kevlar and carbon-fibre/foam sandwich hull and stripped-out interior. Blake thought she could be made competitive, particularly if Duchemin stayed on. He proved his point in the second race of the Cup when, in a reasonable breeze in the Solent, *Lady Be* and *Shockwave* had a great race together to finish third and fourth; in the other races light winds put bigger boats like them out of the running.

The saw-tooth forward edge to the Kevlar reinforcement of her mainsail is a design to spread the loading to avoid a 'gutter' forming ahead of the battens. It was a design first used by John Oakeley, which he called his 'Compensator' sails. Oakeley's rivals smiled benignly on it, but when he used it he didn't have the advantage of Kevlar.

Panda

Name of yacht:–	PANDA
Registered:	United Kingdom 1985
Owner:	P. Whipp
Skipper:	P. Whipp
Designer:	P. Briand
Builder:	Green Marine
Materials:	
PVC Foam/Glass/Kevlar/Carbon/Epoxy	
Launched:	1985
Length o/a:	12.00 metres
Beam:	3.46 metres
Draft:	2.2 metres
Displacement:	5,603 kilos
Rating:	30.5 feet IOR
Sails by:	North/Sobstad
Sail area:	100 sq.metres

There could hardly have been a smile on the face of any of *Panda*'s crew as they set off into the teeth of a gale at the start of the 1985 Fastnet Race. They knew what privations were in store for them and these were not eased by the weather.

Owner/skipper/navigator Peter Whipp is a hard man who accepts no frills in his effort to win races. Nothing that produces speed is missing from his boats, but the interiors are stark to the point where even the Spartans would have turned up their noses. The crew knew therefore that, while there was a stove on board to conform with the

regulations, it would not be used while they were at sea. They knew too that the amount of food on board was down to a bare minimum and that there was really only one place where any of them would be allowed to sleep, however briefly, and that was on the weather rail.

This may not be everyone's idea of a pleasant regimen, but when that crew crossed the finishing line in Plymouth the smiles were the widest of any. They had won the race, and with it the Fastnet Cup, but for Whipp it was the Navigator's Trophy that gave him the greatest satisfaction of all.

Swankers

Having fun is what the builders of Swans conceive to be the principal criterion when they plan their boats. They believe that it can come in a variety of ways, from winning races to cruising in unmitigated luxury, and if they are able to combine the two, so much the better for their customers. It was that sort of philosophy which attracted the owners of *Swankers*, Bill and Mandy Halls and Tony and Lesley Warren, to invest in a Swan 51 for their Cygnet Yacht Charter company.

As this picture all too readily displays, they enjoy their sailing to the limit, as they were prepared to do from the very start when they went to Finland to collect *Swankers* from the builder's yard. Immediately they gained a taste of sailing exhilaration by overtaking all the steamer traffic in the southern Baltic.

The Swan 51 was developed from *Blizzard* (designed by German Frers), one of the British Admiral's Cup team of 1979, and was the first of the Swans from this designer. The first one out of the moulds, *Scoundrel*, was quick to show her paces. In the first race of the 1981 Cup trials she beat *Blizzard* handily. Since then, more than thirty-five have been constructed in a variety of configurations, and one of the latest was specially shortened to 49.98 ft overall for Harry Harkimo to compete in Class II of the BOC Around Alone, the singlehanded race around the world. His *Belmont Finland* suffered none of the damage that many of his competitors did and he was always among the front-runners of the smaller class. She had been specially prepared for the race at the builder's yard in Pietarsaari with added crash bulkheads to conform to the race regulations.

Name of yacht:–	SWANKERS
Registered:	United Kingdom 1983
Owner:	Cygnet Yacht Charters
Skipper:	W. Halls
Designer:	G. Frers
Builder:	Nautor
Materials:	GRP
Launched:	1982
Length o/a:	15.62 metres
Length w/l:	12.92 metres
Beam:	4.49 metres
Draft:	2.70 metres
Displacement:	19,000 kilos
Rating:	39.1 feet IOR
Sails by:	Hood
Sail area:	395.1 sq.metres

L'Esprit d'Equipe

Name of yacht:	L'ESPRIT D'EQUIPE
Registered:	France 1985
Owner:	ACPN
Skipper:	L. Pean
Designer:	P. Briand
Builder:	Chantier Dufour
Materials:	Aluminium
Launched:	1981
Length o/a:	17.56 metres
Beam:	4.84 metres
Displacement:	15,241 kilos
Rating:	46.5 feet IOR
Sails by:	Sobstad
Sail area:	200 sq.metres

There can be no finer example of how a crew take a boat — a relatively ordinary boat — and, by their own efforts, win major races than that afforded by *L'Esprit d'Equipe*. How appropriately named was this 58-footer which won the 1985—86 Whitbread Round the World Race. The name literally means 'Team Spirit', and in fact what Lionel Pean and his seven — sometimes eight − man crew achieved was quite phenomenal.

It was not as though they had a new boat at their disposal. *L'Esprit d'Equipe* began life in 1981 as *33 Export* and started in the previous Whitbread race. She lost her mast on Leg 2 and put into the remote Kerguelen Islands under jury rig. Then, because a new mast could not be flown out, the boat was shipped back to France.

Pean, after a major refit, added a new, heavier keel before setting out to prove his boat by racing her in the Route of Discovery Race, from Spain to the West Indies, and the SORC. It gave him some idea of the modifications which would be necessary before the main event. Those completed, he competed in the Fastnet and beat his fellow-competitors for the Whitbread, moving to become the bookmakers' favourite.

L'Esprit d'Equipe won the first leg but dropped a day to be second on the next, when *Philips Innovator* took the lead. During the Auckland stopover the mast was strengthened to take the compression loadings which the kicker applied to the gooseneck area, but deep in the Southern Ocean on Leg 3 the mast cracked below deck. The team spirit came to the fore and after sails had been doused a repair, using some spare extrusion and considerable ingenuity with Spanish windlasses, was effected. *L'Esprit d'Equipe* went on to win that leg and the next to take the overall corrected time prize and the Whitbread Trophy.

Locura

Ted Turner said, shortly after his *Tenacious* had won the Fastnet Cup in 1979, that he was retiring from offshore racing to 'do something serious with my life — I can't play around all the time'. It was a serious statement of commitment, and one which would have taken a lot for him to revoke.

Locura, then, must have been something of a special yacht, for her owner, George de Guardiola, managed to persuade Turner to join his crew for the 1983 Admiral's Cup. The King of the one-liners was quick in his own defence: 'Retire? — sure I said I was going to retire, but I didn't mean retire forever!' The serious phase was in abeyance; Turner was out to play again.

Locura was designed by Mark Soverel and built by him using an E-glass/Klegecell sandwich. During the SORC, which formed the United States trials that year, she won class D. A 43-footer rating 33.7 ft, she perhaps needed more wind than was generally available that August. Soverel was helmsman, while Turner took his turn offshore and kept his eyes open as tactician for the inshore races. Together with their team-mate *Scarlett O'Hara*, they got it very right in the second race, when they finished first and second and the United States was top team of the day. Then the wind faded and the little boats had a field day at the expense of the Americans.

Turner was not quietened. After a relatively light-wind Fastnet, he reminded everyone that if it had always been as light as this the British might well be speaking Spanish. He had used this allusion (to the Armada being blown away) at the end of the race four years earlier.

Name of yacht:–	LOCURA
Registered:	United States of America 1983
Owner:	G. de Guardiola
Skipper:	G. de Guardiola
Designer:	Soverel
Builder:	Soverel
Materials:	E-Glass/Klegecell
Launched:	1983
Length o/a:	13.00 metres (42ft 8in)
Beam:	4.01 metres (13ft 2in)
Draft:	2.39 metres (7ft 10in)
Displacement:	8,010 kilos (17,646 lb)
Rating:	33.7 feet IOR
Sails by:	Sobstad

Midnight Sun

Name of yacht:–	MIDNIGHT SUN
Registered:	Sweden 1979
Owner:	J. Pehrsson
Designer:	R. Holland
Builder:	Huisman
Materials:	Aluminium
Launched:	1979
Length o/a:	15.30 metres
Beam:	4.37 metres
Draft:	2.50 metres
Displacement:	14,129 kilos
Rating:	39.3 feet IOR
Sails by:	North

Colourful is as colourful does… and there's not a great deal more colourful than *Midnight Sun* as she runs downwind on the only good day of the 1979 Admiral's Cup, the striping of her topsides reflected in the spinnaker and blooper. The 50-ft Ron Holland design was new that year, almost straight out of Wolter Huisman's yard in Holland; aluminium-built, naturally.

Maybe it was because she was so new that Jan Pehrsson's boat was not strictly competitive; there are many things to co-ordinate before a boat of this size gets into the groove. Only occasionally did her crew show that she did have the potential, in the Channel Race perhaps, but then the small boats came in with a rush to make a mockery of their handicaps. By the following year, however, she was fast enough to win the Round Gotland Race against more opponents than she would find almost anywhere else, and to be the top inshore boat in the Sardinia Cup.

In 1981 *Midnight Sun* went to the SORC, where she was expected to do well. She was, however, attacked by pirates while in Caribbean waters and, while she escaped without any loss of life to her crew, they decided to opt out. One cannot seriously blame them.

She was sufficiently interesting to Jean-Louis Fabry — who had finally retired his four-time French team boat, *Revolution* — to persuade him to charter her for the French Admiral's Cup team of 1981 after another Round Gotland win. It was a ploy which appeared to work when the wind blew at all. A fourth in the second inshore race was followed by a win in the Channel Race, an event which Fabry appears to treat as his own property, judging by the number of times he has won it in class or outright.

Then *Midnight Sun* sparkled in the third inshore race for the Champagne Mumm Trophy; finishing seventh she was by far the best of the big boats. The wind then fizzled out for the Fastnet, and with it the effervescence of *Midnight Sun*.

Marionette IX

Name of yacht:-	MARIONETTE IX
Registered:	United Kingdom 1986
Owner:	C. Dunning
Skipper:	C. Dunning
Designer:	R. Humphreys/E. Dubois
Builder:	K. Bushe
Materials:	Kevlar/Carbon/Foam
Launched:	1985
Length o/a:	13.41 metres
Length w/l:	10.36 metres
Beam:	4.27 metres
Draft:	2.44 metres
Displacement:	7,938 kilos
Rating:	34 feet IOR
Sails by:	North/Sobstad
Sail area:	97.55 sq.metres

As the masts of ocean-racing yachts have tended to climb nearer to the clouds there has been a noted reluctance among their designers to do anything to make them skinnier. More and more spreaders have been added with their relative cross-bracing rigging rods so that a seagull flying close by might have difficulty in avoiding being shredded by them. In a fore and aft plane the mast relies on many movables for its stability.

It is here that things can go wrong since the balance of the forces has to be kept in equilibrium. The forestay, by the International Offshore Rule, is fixed but the topmast backstay and the running backstays of a fractional rig are not. And when a spinnaker is hoisted there are other loads which come into play — the thrust of the spinnaker boom against the mast, the tension of the inner forestay (if one is fitted) and the effect of the boom and mainsail.

On this breezy Cowes Week day of 1986, *Marionette IX* was the first to hoist her spinnaker and, in the words of her crew, 'was not pushed to lay the mark'. They were the best and were the pathfinders — until the boom end went skyward. The loss of the boom's forward pressure on the mast allowed the thrust of the spinnaker boom to invert the mast's bend. Without gaining tension on the boom vang — and it was the failure of the hydraulics which caused the skying — the only solution lay in tripping the spinnaker from the end of its pole.

The bowman rushed forward, climbed up on to the pulpit and had his hand on the snap shackle when the mast gave way. It was Wednesday and just six days later the boat had to be shipped to the Sardinia Cup. Proctors completed the rebuild of the spar in time and the story has its happy ending. Chris Dunning and *Marionette IX* led the British team to a first-ever victory in this Mediterranean equivalent of the Admiral's Cup. On that Wednesday in Cowes Week the victory would have seemed impossible as mast, boom, sails and rigging lay over the side.

Mistress Quickly

Name of yacht:–	MISTRESS QUICKLY
Registered:	Bermuda 1980
Owner:	W. Whitehouse-Vaux
Designer:	Bob Miller
Builder:	Halvorsen, Morson and Gowland
Materials:	Aluminium
Launched:	1974
Length o/a:	22.07 metres (72ft 5in)
Length w/l:	20.27 metres (66ft 6in)
Beam:	4.43 metres (14ft 6in)
Draft:	3.23 metres (10ft 7in)
Displacement:	29,443 kilos (64,863 lb)
Rating:	67.1 feet IOR
Sails by:	Hood
Sail area:	241.5 sq.metres (2,600 sq.feet)

In 1979, *Mistress Quickly* won the first Fort Lauderdale—Key West race outright, and the prize for that race was a 'designer' spinnaker. No one in the race committee had foreseen that it would be won by so large a boat, or envisaged the subsequent happenings. One of the options open to the winner was that he could choose whichever sailmaker he desired. Bill Whitehouse-Vaux chose Hood, and then, after discussions with an artist, he proceeded to choose the pattern. One thing, however, went wrong. After the first spinnaker was made, the dye ran and a second one had to be made. The prize the following year was limited in size to boats of under Three-quarter-Ton rating!

Ben Lexcen (when he was still Bob Miller) designed this boat, as *Ballyhoo*, for Jack Rooklyn in 1974, and she was campaigned widely by him. It was not until after Rooklyn had sold her to Bill Whitehouse-Vaux that the boat, with the name changed, began to achieve a great popularity among the sailors. It has made her, and the parties associated with her, legendary.

The 72-footer was built by Halvorsen, Morson and Gowland in aluminium shortly after they had built the first-ever aluminium 12-Metre, *Southern Cross*. She chased the line honours in Australia before heading for Europe and a first across the line in the 1977, light-weather, Fastnet.

After that she was sold and since then she has raced on both sides of the Atlantic, always being a potential corrected-time winner. *Mistress Quickly* still holds the elapsed time record for the Middle Sea Race and for the Round the Island Race. A list of her alumni reads like a *Who's Who* of yachting, and she will forever hold a fond place in many of their hearts. Her role now is one of cruising, the Mediterranean in the summer and the Caribbean in the winter; and a few fun regattas.

Outsider

One of the few boats to be chosen twice for the Admiral's Cup and to win it on the second time around, *Outsider* started life as *Dusselboot*, one of the first designs to come out of the partnership of Friedrich Judel and Rolf Vrolijk and built in aluminium alloy by Yachtafenwerft.

The minimum rater (30 ft IOR) soon made a name for herself in Britain when she won the Round the Island Race in 1981 on a day when the German team gave notice of its strength, *Pinta* and *Container* finishing fifth and seventh. *Dusselboot* won that day because she was able to hitch a tow on the quarter wave of the Swan 51 *Scoundrel* from the Needles to St Catherine's Point, the crew's faces smiling the while.

That year the German team was third, a position which might have been improved at least to second had not *Dusselboot* lost her mast in the Channel Race. The name-change came when she was bought by Tilmar Hansen, and after she was tweaked and improved she made the team for Cowes again. This time the team was totally dominant and consistently good — there were only eight points between top and bottom boats in the team, and they were 167 clear of Italy in second place.

On this day of black skies and barbed lightning in Christchurch Bay there were dramatic changes in the strength and direction of the wind. *Outsider* was one of the many to be caught with too much sail up at one point, and her crew struggled to get one headsail off and a much smaller one set in its place.

Name of yacht:—	OUTSIDER
Registered:	Germany 1983
Owner:	T. Hansen
Skipper:	T. Reff
Designer:	Judel/Vrolijk
Builder:	Yachtafenwerft
Materials:	Aluminium
Launched:	1981
Length o/a:	11.9 metres
Beam:	3.83 metres
Draft:	2.3 metres
Displacement:	5,769 kilos
Rating:	30 feet IOR
Sails by:	North

Paragon

Name of yacht:–	PARAGON
Registered:	United Kingdom 1985
Owner:	M. Whipp
Skipper:	M. Whipp
Designer:	A. Thompson
Builder:	Thompson/Feloy
Materials:	Kevlar/Carbon/Epoxy
Launched:	1985
Length o/a:	18.29 metres
Length w/l:	17.98 metres
Beam:	14.33 metres
Draft:	3.35 metres/1.07 metres
Displacement:	4,082 kilos
Rating:	Formula II multihull
Sails by:	Hood
Sail area:	232.25 sq.metres

The yellow, triple-fingered form of *Paragon* slices like a three-bladed knife through the water, perhaps the fastest ever sailing boat of 60 ft. She was designed and built by Adrian Thompson for Michael Whipp with much attention to aerodynamic cleanness.

Thompson constructed *Paragon* of pre-preg Kevlar with carbon-fibre and R-Glass reinforcement using epoxy resin. Her all-up sailing weight is little over 10,000 lb. The floats have a 200 per cent buoyancy, and tremendous stability is achieved by her 47-ft beam. This has also caused problems since it places tremendous strain on the crossbeams, particularly where they attach to the floats, and breaking up in this area caused her retirement from the 1985 Round Britain Race, when she was leading on the leg from Lerwick to Lowestoft, and from the Round Europe Race the same year.

Where she has been able to display her full potential is in round-the-buoys racing, particularly at the 1986 La Trinité Trophy des Multicoques. She was starting at the same time as the 85-footers and spent most of her time beating them home. In the first race she arrived at the starting line nine minutes late and caught all but two, while in the other three races she was first home ahead of *Roger & Gallet*, *Charente Maritime* and *Royale*. Where she was able to gain most ground was in tacking. *Paragon* took about 25 seconds to go about while the big catamarans were anything up to a minute and a half before they were underway again, the light weight of the trimaran giving her better acceleration than the maxi-cats.

Upwind *Paragon* can obtain 16 knots and has a tacking angle of 85 degrees, far better than any of the cats or equivalent trimarans. Much of the upwind efficiency is due to the rig with its rotating alloy Proctor mast.

In the 1986 Silk Cut Multihull Challenge race from Brighton to London, *Paragon* was hit by a coaster. She managed to limp into port despite severe damage, whilst the coaster ploughed on without stopping. Mike Whipp's helmsman accompanying him on the race was Rodney Pattisson, and it was he who telephoned his friend, sailmaker John McWilliams. McWilliams picked them up in his light aeroplane and they went on to search the east-coast ports of Great Britain, looking for a coaster painted green to match the scars left on *Paragon*! At the time of going to press, a ship bearing yellow paint scratches just off the bow was having 'legal difficulties'…

12-Metres

The fascination of 12-Metres is hypnotic. From whichever angle they are viewed, they have a beauty that is all their own. From above, each boat's eleven crewmen can be seen scurrying about like ants, for they are grossly understaffed and, if anyone should doubt the athleticism of yacht racing, they should try a race as crewman aboard a Twelve in 25 knots of breeze. They should consider the work to be done at an overcrowded leeward mark with genoas to go up and spinnakers to come down, all in the twinkling of a eye, while those at the back have the problems of planning the strategy and pointing the boat in the right direction.

The 12-Metre World Championship off Fremantle, twelve months before the 1987 America's Cup, provided the class's aficionados with more than a foretaste of what sailing a 12-Metre would be like in February; it provided them with a never-to-be-forgotten spectacle, and at the same time gave the organizers the opportunity to test their facilities under working conditions. It also gave the syndicates some idea of where they stood globally.

No one who was there will ever forget the sight of fourteen 12-Metres coming to a starting-line or of them crowded together around the turning marks; that was simply majestic. Nowhere had there been that number of modern Twelves racing together before, and it was racing enjoyed by all those who took part, as much as anything because it was so very different to the incessant practice to which they had been subjected, and it was anything but match racing. Very few had ever experienced level racing in boats of this size, and it unearthed some shortcomings.

Peculiarly it was shown that the winner, *Australia III*, was off the pace in heavier breezes and that the Alan Bond syndicate would have to come up with a newer, faster boat to have any chance of defending the Cup which *Australia II* had won. And how the Taskforce syndicate must have felt a year later about the lost opportunity to discover that it, too, had a shortage of speed with the *Kookaburra*s; there will always be the argument, though, that if Dennis Conner had taken part he would have won that 1986 Championship so easily that he would have taken the fire out of all the others.

Speculation was rife among the spectators anyway, but they really had value for their money out on Gage Roads, where the world's most exacting preview in yachting was also the most spectacularly exciting.

Pocket Battleship

She was to be the first of the 'sponsored' IOR boats in Britain under the name of *Vodafone Venturer* but the RORC would not relax the rule for 1985 and the Dubois/ Humphreys 44-footer became *Pocket Battleship* instead. Her owner, Martin Gibson, felt that there was a place for the bigger type of boat in the Admiral's Cup, but in her first year the masthead-rigged craft ran into some problems.

The first came very early in her career when she was out practising in the western Solent before the season was fully underway. In a fresh breeze she was running under spinnaker and preparing for a gybe when she broached violently. For a second she gave a full view of her keel as the masthead hit the water and then she hung there on her side until a shroud gave way and the mast snapped in two. Immediately the boat came upright, but there was a full week's work needed to have her ready for the following weekend.

Pocket Battleship was a very powerful yacht which revelled in a breeze but tended to 'stick' in the lighter winds. She failed to make the British team and was chartered to Singapore, the team placed sixth overall, and made a better than average showing in a year when the small boats were supreme.

For 1986, there were some alterations to the hull and a new bulbed keel was fitted to give her greater stability for a lighter weight. *Pocket Battleship* was then chosen for the Sardinia Cup and was a member of the first team, with *Full Pelt* and *Marionette IX*, to bring that trophy to British shores.

Police Car

Name of yacht:–	POLICE CAR
Registered:	Australia 1979
Owner:	P. Cantwell
Designer:	E. Dubois
Builder:	S. Ward
Materials:	Aluminium
Launched:	1979
Length o/a:	12.95 metres
Length w/l:	9.91 metres
Beam:	3.68 metres
Draft:	2.17 metres
Rating:	32 feet IOR
Sails by:	Hood
Sail area:	81.75 sq.metres

Peter Cantwell asked Ed Dubois to design him a fresh-wind flyer to the Two-Ton limit of 32 ft IOR, and *Police Car* was everything he could have desired. She won the Australian Admiral's Cup trials in Melbourne when the wind gave her every opportunity to extend herself, particularly downwind in breezes over 20 knots, but then found conditions at the 1979 Two Ton Cup in Poole an anathema; light and shifting winds were far from her forte.

What she needed, and what she got at the Admiral's Cup a month later, were the strongest-ever winds for that event. The fractional-rigged *Police Car* loved the Solent races with the reaches and runs against the tide multiplying her advantage. She was top boat of the top team that year, and no one was surprised; only *Eclipse* was able to beat her for the highest overall points. In the gale-tossed Fastnet Race, *Police Car* had a wild and wet ride under boomed-out staysail, reefed main and storm jib for a while, then piled on the canvas as the wind lightened to finish fourth of the Admiral's Cuppers.

Jim Hardy, who was aboard *Impetuous* for that series, was much impressed by the Dubois design and bought her to race mainly in Australian waters. Twice, in 1980 and 1982, he took her to win her division in the Sydney–Hobart Race and he also competed in the Clipper Cup in Hawaii where the boat lost her mast, folded at the gooseneck. There was a spare bottom section and, after it was clear that the boat was going to be back in for the next race, Sir James (by then he had been knighted) remarked that the new bottom piece would have to be painted. 'What colour?' came the question. 'Oh, pink'll do,' said the yachting knight. Next morning it was there in its resplendent hue — the rest, of course, was pale blue!

Pro-Motion

Many are the owners who now believe that the spartan approach to racing has gone just a little too far, although they realize the need to keep unnecessary weight out of the boat. They know too that there is little chance of any series production cruiser/racer winning races in the Grand Prix division but they always hope that there can be a compromise of sorts.

Bénéteau sensed the climate as they increased the size of their range of cruiser/racers. They had too the background of producing a limited series of pure racing boats, their One-Tonners particularly, and it seemed right for them to foray into a larger type of boat. The top end of the Admiral's Cup rating band looked singularly appropriate.

Pro-Motion was one of the first two Bénéteau 51s to come off the production line, and her prettiness produced some envious gasps when she turned up at Cowes Week in 1986. Her dark blue topsides gleamed, and her speed through the water matched her grace. It was as though a dream had come true for her owner, Bert Dolk; a comfortable boat with a more than rudimentary accommodation plan below.

Like Wictor Forss' *Carat*, her sister ship, *Pro-Motion* is a racing version of the Bénéteau 51. The deck layout — strictly a racing format — belies the relative comfort available below. There is an owner's cabin aft with its own shower and head, while the crew's comfort has not been neglected either; it is as though there has been a return to the live-aboard racing boat of the 1960s.

Pro-Motion and her sisters have yet to prove themselves in the upper echelon of racing, but their pedigree is exceptional. Designed by German Frers as a logical development from *Fujimo, Nitissima* and *Morning Star*, they should have little difficulty in holding their own.

Name of yacht:–	PRO-MOTION
Registered:	Holland 1986
Owner:	B. Dolk
Skipper:	B. Dolk
Designer:	G. Frers
Builder:	Bénéteau
Materials:	Carbon/Kevlar/Divinycell
Launched:	1986
Length o/a:	15.20 metres
Length w/l:	12.53 metres
Beam:	4.51 metres
Draft:	2.75 metres
Displacement:	12,500 kilos
Rating:	39.6 feet IOR
Sails by:	North

Sanction

Name of yacht:–	SANCTION
Registered:	United Kingdom 1983
Owner:	J. Morris
Skipper:	J. Morris
Designer:	S. Jones
Builder:	Woof Boats
Materials:	S – Glass/Carbon fibre/foam
Launched:	1982
Length o/a:	14.38 metres
Length w/l:	11.58 metres
Beam:	4.21 metres
Draft:	2.63 metres
Displacement:	10,017 kilos
Rating:	35.2 feet IOR
Sails by:	Hood/Sobstad
Sail area:	114.5 sq.metres

'Raw garlic and bread' is how Bill Green remembers the diet aboard *Sanction* towards the end of the long race of the 1982 Sardinia Cup. The race — which was the longest Sardinia Cup race on record in terms of time taken — was an almost total disaster for the 47-ft Stephen Jones design which was one of the Swiss team.

It was one of those merry-go-rounds of fate for *Sanction*'s crew. On the way out to the start there was a fire in the electrics and they had to make do without any instrumentation for the whole 360 miles. Then the wind decided that its presence was not needed and

before they reached Porto Cervo both the food and the cooking gas ran out, leaving only stale bread and the odd clove of garlic to stave off the pangs of hunger.

That race was perhaps a reflection of the boat's career; one which was not totally happy. She was late from her builders, and then underwent many modifications in the course of her racing life, including the fitting of a space frame to take the rig and keel loads and a new keel. Before she was laid up, *Sanction* became the front-runner at the Lymington Winter Series, with Chris Law steering her.

White Crusader

A month late was how anyone would describe the British challenge for the America's Cup in 1987 — the development of *White Crusader* was always running one month behind. And she wasn't the boat which the Royal Thames syndicate had planned to use in the first place. There had been even less time to develop the radical Twelve designed by David Hollom, and so the evolutionary Ian Howlett design took on the front-line role.

White Crusader was a boat which every syndicate expected to make the semi-finals of the challenger trials. She was meticulously prepared for the third

round-robin with an optimization programme that included a new bow, prefabricated in England and flown in, alterations to the hanging of the keel and modifications to its wing shape, moving the rudder aft and trimming the underside of the counter. The changes brought significant improvements in speed, but still *White Crusader* lost races which she should have won and didn't make the final four.

Nevertheless, she did ensure that Britain was kept at the forefront of America's Cup technology, and next time...

Name of yacht:–	WHITE CRUSADER
Registered:	United Kingdom 1986
Owner: British America's Cup Challenges PLC	
Skipper:	H. Cudmore
Designer:	I. Howlett
Builder:	Cougar Marine
Materials:	Aluminium
Launched:	1986
Length o/a:	19.90 metres
Beam:	3.80 metres
Draft:	2.70 metres
Rating:	12 Metre class
Sails by:	North

Stars & Stripes

Name of yacht:–	STARS & STRIPES
Registered:	United States of America 1986
Owner:	Sail America Foundation
Skipper:	D. Conner
Designer:	B. Chance/B. Nelson/D. Pedrick
Builder:	R. Derecktor Inc/Gereghty Marine Inc.
Materials:	Aluminium
Launched:	1986
Length o/a:	20.5 metres (67ft 3in)
Length w/l:	14.5 metres (47ft 7in)
Beam:	3.8 metres (12ft 6in)
Draft:	2.8 metres (9ft 2in)
Displacement:	30,000 kilos (66,090 lb)
Rating:	12 Metre class
Sails by:	Sobstad/North/Sail America
Sail area:	168 sq.metres (1,808 sq.feet)

There is no motivation quite as powerful as revenge, and that was deep-seated in the heart of Dennis Conner when he began his three-year plan to return the America's Cup to his native shores. He had made a mistake in underestimating the technology of the Australians, and lost the America's Cup on that fateful day, 26 September 1983. It rankled, and Conner became 'Big Bad Dennis', the Californian bear with a sore head, a mean character who was to show no mercy.

The technological failure of 1983 was duly noted, and no less than three designers were invited to co-ordinate their efforts under John Marshall, who would also seek the input of scientists from the leading corporations of the United States, including Boeing and Ford and the aerospace agency, NASA. Even then, Conner was heard to say that they had only scratched the surface of modern technology to produce the fastest 12-Metre in the world.

When he lost races in the second round-robin of the challenger trials there were all too many prepared to write Conner off. He admitted later that he had been 'sandbagging'. 'We didn't show all our cards in the beginning,' he remarked after the Cup was won. He was still experimenting, but it became all too clear that that part of the campaign was over when *Stars & Stripes* met *USA* in the semi-final and Conner blew the doors off his arch-rival, Tom Blackaller, in four straight races. Only a small gear failure stopped him from repeating the exercise with the New Zealanders in the final, and he won the Louis Vuitton Cup by 4–1.

After trailing for two days with *Kookaburra III*, the New Zealanders came ashore to tell everyone to prepare for San Diego, but even they would have found it hard to predict just how easily *Stars & Stripes* would win back the America's Cup. Iain Murray, *Kookaburra III*'s skipper, put it at two-tenths of a knot of extra speed to windward. However much it was, it was more than enough for a whitewash.

Revolution

There will probably never be another yacht quite like *Revolution*, which raced in four Admiral's Cups and was still in the prizes to the end. It was a boat which was so very different to all the others and inspired the then guru of offshore designers, Dick Carter, to remark when he first saw her, 'Pop art has come to yachting.'

In any marina she was the ugly duckling in a sea of swans; her fat red hull with its huge, broad transom was as out of place as a pre-fab in the Royal Crescent at Bath. Her owner, Jean-Louis Fabry, had given Group Finot a free hand to design him a fast boat, but even he must have blanched when he first saw what they were to offer. However this light-displacement tearaway had the ability to disappear from bigger boats downwind and the potential to go upwind faster than any boat of her kind had ever done before. She was little more than a dinghy with a lid and there was very little concession to comfort down below.

Built by Wolter Huisman in aluminium alloy, *Revolution* was launched on 29 December 1972, and was the first Admiral's Cupper in the Channel Race the next year. It was the start of something which was to become quite a habit. While her record was not strong in the next two years, it was in 1976 that Fabry began an assault on the RORC trophies. With four wins in class, *Revolution* won her first RORC championship in 1976 and the following year repeated that and took the Yacht of the Year and Alan Paul Trophies as well.

In 1978, *Revolution* was only entered in four RORC races, the Cervantes Trophy, the du Guingand Bowl, the Morgan Cup and the Channel Race, and won them all. It gave her a third RORC Class II championship as well as the Yacht of the Year and Alan Paul Trophies for the second successive year. Her fourth Admiral's Cup selection, in 1979, saw her move down a class, but she won that for her fourth RORC championship.

Name of yacht:–	REVOLUTION
Registered:	France 1979
Owner:	J-L. Fabry
Skipper:	J-L. Fabry
Designer:	Finot
Builder:	Huisman
Materials:	Aluminium
Launched:	1972
Length o/a:	11.81 metres
Beam:	3.93 metres
Draft:	2.03 metres
Rating:	29.5 feet IOR
Sails by:	Banks

Roger & Gallet

Name of yacht:–	ROGER & GALLET
Registered:	France 1986
Owner:	Roger & Gallet
Skipper:	E. Loizeau
Designer:	S. Langevin
Builder:	ACX/Maas Hurel
Materials:	Airex/Nida carbon sandwich
Launched:	1984
Length o/a:	23 metres
Length w/l:	20 metres
Beam:	12.50 metres
Displacement:	6,400 kilos
Rating:	Formula I multihull
Sails by:	Techniques Voiles/Crudennec
Sail area:	327 sq.metres

The search for speed in offshore boats among the French very soon led to an argument as to whether two hulls or three was the most efficient design. Concern for safety parameters led to the initial surge along the trimaran path but the need for more speed saw the rapid introduction of catamarans into the racing fleet. Their size began to increase, and with it their sophistication; there was also a vast improvement in the top speeds achieved by these boats. Having said that, the transatlantic record is held, in 1987, by the 75ft trimaran *Fleury Michon*.

Royale's previous transatlantic record, in turn breaking that of *Jet Services*, had proved that prolonged speed was possible; the 24 hours during which Mike Birch and his crew sailed *Formule Tag* for 524 miles may not remain in the record books for much longer, the way such craft are progressing. Those were all straight-line sailing records but a shorter one of *Roger & Gallet*'s is just as significant. During the 1986 Southampton Multihull Grand Prix she went east about the Isle of Wight in just under four hours. The following day the 75-ft catamaran knocked a few more minutes off her own record for the same course in 3 hours 42 minutes 5 seconds.

This amazing boat was built in several different factories and assembled in Brest. The main beam was constructed in carbon fibre by an aircraft company in Paris which baked the fibres in an autoclave, while the hulls, of an Airex foam/carbon fibre sandwich, were made in Holland. The result was the lightest-ever offshore racing catamaran of her size, and it was this attention to the reduction of weight by her designer, Serge Langevin, which ensured high speeds for *Roger & Gallet*. It was Uffa Fox, after all, who once remarked that weight was only of use in a steamroller; he would certainly have approved of this boat.

In the 1987 Round Europe Race, *Roger & Gallet* met her Waterloo and was capsized in heavy weather off Cape Finisterre in Spain, on the leg from Lorient to Vilamoura in Portugal. Fortunately there was no loss of life and the boat was salvaged, minus her rig.

Royale

The fascination of speed under sail has gripped men ever since they laid aside the paddles of their coracles to blow themselves across the river, and there is no more fascinating record than that of the transatlantic crossing from the Ambrose Light at the entrance to New York Harbour to the Lizard at the south-western tip of Cornwall. For 75 years the 12 days four hours record of the schooner *Atlantic* and of her skipper Charlie Barr had stood the test of time, but then came the multihulls and an average of 10 knots was no longer enough.

By 1984, Patrick Morvan had raised it to 15.16 knots when he made the crossing in the 60-ft catamaran *Jet Services*, taking 8 days 16 hours and 36 minutes. Bigger boats, it was argued, could do it quicker and *Royale*, an 85-footer designed by Group Graal, was one to make the attempt. Mike Birch's *Tag* had shown the way with a 524-mile day and co-skippers Philippe Facque and Loic Caradec bided their time in New York in 1986 until the right set of weather conditions were forecast before making their attempt.

Using Jean-Yves Bernot, their computer-routing specialist ashore in France as their guide, Facque and Caradec with four other crew beat the record by nineteen-and-a-half hours. Their crossing took 7 days 21 hours and 5 minutes, an average speed of 16.29 knots; their best 24-hour run was 468 miles. It was a magnificent effort. The current record holder is the 75-ft trimaran *Fleury Michon*, just 8¼ hours quicker.

Later in 1986 the joy turned to tragedy when Caradec took the boat in the single-handed Route de Rhum race. *Royale* was found upside down 300 miles off the French coast by fellow-competitor Florence Arthaud. Of Caradec there was no sign. He had paid the ultimate price in his search for further glory and his lust for speed.

Name of yacht:–	ROYALE
Registered:	France 1986
Owner:	Coursocean
Skipper:	L. Caradec/P. Facque
Designer:	Group Graal
Builder:	Multiplast/Agencement Marine
Materials:	Airex/Carbon/Kevlar/Glass
Launched:	1983
Length o/a:	25.90 metres
Length w/l:	24.90 metres
Beam:	12.00 metres
Draft:	3.00 metres/0.6 metres
Displacement:	10,000 kilos
Rating:	Formula I multihull
Sails by:	Technique Voiles
Sail area:	345 sq.metres + 65 sq.metre mast

Vagrant

Name of yacht:–	VAGRANT
Registered:	United Kingdom 1987
Owner:	P. de Savary
Skipper:	D. Romcke
Designer:	N. Herreshoff
Builder:	Herreshoff Boatyard, Rhode Island
Materials:	Wood
Launched:	1910
Length o/a:	32.5 metres
Length w/l:	18 metres
Beam:	5.5 metres
Draft:	3.5 metres
Displacement:	71,123 kilos
Sails by:	North
Sail area:	400 sq.metres

Peter de Savary's lovely schooner, photographed under every inch of sail in the Solent during Cowes Week, 1987, has an interesting history. In 1910 Nathanael Herreshoff, the famous American designer of so many grand yachts — including six America's Cup defenders between 1893 and 1920 — was commissioned by the Vanderbilts to design a schooner for Harold, heir to the family fortune. She was built that year in the Herreshoff yard at Bristol, Rhode Island and was raced to first place in the Bermuda Race the same season.

In 1912 she was sold to Hendon Chubb who renamed her *Queen Mab*. Over the next forty years she was cruised and raced by a succession of owners, but from 1953 to 1971 she was raced regularly by Larry Pringle and Phyllis Brunson, notching up nine TransPacific Races where she acquitted herself well against such competitors as

Ondine, *Ticonderoga* and *Windward Passage*.

In 1983 she turned up in Antigua in poor condition, and was taken over by Hans Lammers, a young Dutchman who semi-restored her. He changed her name back to the original *Vagrant* and started chartering her, but disaster struck in 1984 when a sudden storm dismasted and disabled her. Lammers limped back to Antigua under engine.

Vagrant was saved from an ignominious end, rotting in the sun, by Peter de Savary who set Antigua's shipyard to work. In 20 months, local craftsmen has restored her to the perfection you see here, backed by research into Herreshoff drawings and the rigging skills of Spencer's of Cowes. And to those who have been fortunate enough to see *Vagrant*'s accommodation, she is every bit as lovely below as she is on deck. But then she was designed by Herreshoff.

Virgin Atlantic Challenger II (with Royale)

The ultimate boating record across the Atlantic was for years held by the liners, the *Queen Mary*'s 3 days 20 hours 42 minutes of 1938 finally toppling to the *United States* fourteen years later. She took 3 days 10 hours and 40 minutes for the crossing, and when airliners displaced the vast passenger vessels it appeared that the record was likely to remain for ever.

Not, however, in the minds of men like Richard Branson, a quixotic adventurer in business and one who clearly liked the challenge. His first attempt, with powerboat champion Ted Toleman in a 65-ft catamaran, ended three hours and 138 miles from the Bishop Rock, when *Virgin Atlantic Challenger* hit some floating debris, was holed and sank. Dampened but not dismayed, Branson was keen to try again, but this time Toleman could not help; his Cougar yard was committed to building two aluminium 12-Metres for the British America's Cup challenge. Branson would not be stopped, went to Brooke Marine for a 72-ft monohull and the challenge was on all over again.

The route was carefully planned, and the refuelling rendezvous positioned so that there would be the minimum of delay. Fog and icebergs were the expected early hazards off the North American coast, but neither materialized until, twenty-four hours into the attempt, the fog came. Then at the second refuelling rendezvous water got mixed with the diesel oil and 7½ hours were lost. Fuel filters were in short supply, and that needed an emergency drop of spares from an RAF Nimrod prior to the last refuelling.

Virgin Atlantic Challenger II made her landfall with two hours and nine minutes to spare. The new record stands at 3 days 8 hours and 31 minutes, an average speed of 38.86 knots. Someone is going to have to try for 40 knots; Richard Branson, perhaps?

VIRGIN ATLANTIC CHALLENGER II	
Registered:	United Kingdom 1986
Owner:	Richard Branson
Skipper:	Richard Branson
Designer:	S. Levi
Builder:	Brooke Yachts
Materials:	Aluminium
Launched:	1986
Length o/a:	22.02 metres
Length w/l:	17 metres
Beam:	5.82 metres
Draft:	0.91 metres
Displacement:	31.5 tonnes
Engines: Twin V12 396 TB 93 turbo by MTU	
Engine power:	2000 BHP each

Rucanor Tri Star

Name of yacht:–	RUCANOR TRI STAR
Registered:	Belgium 1985
Owner:	Rijswijk/Rucanor Tri Star
Skipper:	G.Versluys
Designer:	G.Ribadeau Dumas
Builder:	F.Maas
Materials:	Kevlar/Balsa/Carbon
Launched:	1985
Length o/a:	17.66 metres
Length w/l:	14.10 metres
Beam:	4.90 metres
Draft:	2.95 metres
Displacement:	15,559 kilos
Rating:	45.6 feet IOR
Sails by:	Hood
Sail area:	170 sq.metres

Skipper Gustaaf Versluys competed in the third Whitbread race in the 43-ft *Croky*, the smallest boat, and had a long, slow passage around the world. The next time he was determined to have a different trip, and enlisted the sponsorship of the sports goods firm Rucanor early in his plans.

Rucanor commissioned the design of the boat from Guy Ribadeau Dumas and the building from Frans Maas in his Breskens yard. In all other respects it was a Belgian operation for Versluys with his relatively light-displacement yacht which rated at the top end of Division D.

Ribadeau Dumas had incorporated into her design a variable geometry stern, worked by air pressure, which could lift the counter 20cm for downwind sailing or depress it for windward work. Unfortunately, when the boat was almost completed in January 1985, the Offshore Racing Council informed the owners that this novel feature contravened the rules, and for the Whitbread race the stern had to be fixed in one position. The design also incorporated elliptical keel and rudder profiles, and a 2,000-lb bulb was added to the keel to provide greater upwind stability.

The first leg of the race was her worst; she finished 10th of the 14 finishers. But from there on she made some impressive showings. Fifth, third and fifth in fleet on the next three legs gave her first in the race in Division D and fifth overall, 29 hours behind *UBS Switzerland* on corrected time. She was one of the few boats to have almost the same crew for the entire race, adding only one person for each of the Atlantic legs; on the first one it was the sponsor's General Manager, Bastiaan van Rijswijk, who had done much towards managing the project from the outset.

SAILING FOR FLANDERS
HET LAATSTE NIEUWS
Rucanor TriStar
Polymers

Sabina

Designed by Jac de Ridder, *Sabina* was launched in 1981 and failed to make the German team for the Sardinia Cup instead, racing in the Austrian team. The aluminium boat, which was built by Wolter Huisman, was continually improved and the following year was top points scorer in the winning German team in the Admiral's Cup, where her second in the Channel Race and fourth in the Fastnet helped enormously.

Too little attention is paid to racing as a team in these events but here is an excellent example of how that can be utilized. *Sabina* has locked into the stern wave of *Outsider*, which was a slightly faster-reaching boat, and is being dragged along at the same speed as they approach the Australian *Once More Dear Friends*, while crossing the Solent to the mainland shore to sail in the slacker water off Lepe Beach.

As they get closer to *Once More Dear Friends*, the two German boats can climb up on to her wind and begin to slow her by blanketing her sails. Then when they are really close they must choose their moment to get on her leeward quarter wave so that they can jointly establish an inside overlap at the next mark, gaining four points in doing so.

In addition, as they slow down *Once More Dear Friends* they will take her out of the 'towing' influence of their larger team-mate *Pinta*, allowing *Pinta* to go clear away to a better position and save her time on handicap. In 1983 the Germans sailed as though they were fully aware of the advantages of competing *as a team*.

Name of yacht:–	SABINA
Registered:	Germany 1983
Owner:	H.Noach
Designer:	J. de Ridder
Builder:	Huisman
Materials:	Aluminium
Launched:	1981
Length o/a:	12.20 metres
Beam:	3.69 metres
Draft:	2.27 metres
Displacement:	6,040 kilos
Rating:	30 feet IOR

Sayula II

Name of yacht:–	SAYULA II
Registered:	Mexico 1977
Owner:	R. Carlin
Skipper:	R. Carlin
Designer:	Sparkman & Stephens
Builder:	Nautor
Materials:	GRP
Launched:	1972
Length o/a:	19.75 metres
Length w/l:	14.33 metres
Beam:	4.98 metres
Draft:	2.82 metres
Displacement:	25,569 kilos
Rating:	46.8 feet IOR
Sails by:	Hood
Sail area:	166.94 sq.metres

Sayula II was almost exactly halfway between Cape Town and Sydney, about 48.20S, 90.37E, on 24 November 1973 when, as Butch Dalrymple-Smith wrote, 'It is not possible to put adequately into words the feeling you get when your home and world turns from a comfortable microcosm of civilisation into a wreck.' *Sayula II* had capsized.

For Dalrymple-Smith the Led Zeppelin album *Houses of the Holy* will never be the same again. He had just put the tape into the eight-track when 'there was a most almighty crash and the side of the hull leapt towards me'.

Sayula II was on the face of a wave when the falling crest caught the stern first, forcing it down the wave faster than the bow. With the bow gripping the water and the stern in the falling foam, the boat slewed round almost broadside to the wave; and then the wave broke. The boat fell and next hit the water when it was almost upside down. Both men in the cockpit were thrown out, tethered to the boat only by their harnesses, but remarkably the masts were still there. It was a tribute to her builders, Nautor Oy, that the Swan 65 was virtually undamaged; a cracked cabin window, the loss of a couple of compasses and some damage to the mast fittings apart, *Sayula II* was still in one piece.

She had been caught by a freak wave while competing in the first Whitbread Round the World Race with only a storm jib and staysail set. Dalrymple-Smith and Keith Lorence soon had those sails down while the entire crew set about reducing the shambles below deck, finding that the damage was remarkably light. It was twelve hours before the sails, the same ones, were set again and although 24 hours later a spinnaker was set it was generally agreed that it was a week before the boat was being 'raced' again. Nevertheless, *Sayula II* won that second leg and went into the overall lead, one which she did not relinquish. She claimed the Whitbread Trophy when she finished at Portsmouth on Easter Sunday, 1974.

Scoundrel

Name of yacht:–	SCOUNDREL
Registered:	United Kingdom 1980
Owner:	B.Owen
Skipper:	B.Owen
Designer:	G.Frers
Builder:	Nautor
Materials:	GRP
Launched:	1981
Length o/a:	15.62 metres
Length w/l:	12.92 metres
Beam:	4.37 metres
Draft:	2.71 metres
Displacement:	16,507 kilos
Rating:	40.2 feet IOR
Sails by:	North
Sail area:	148 sq.metres

Nautor began a new series of cruiser/ racers, away from their traditional liaison with Sparkman & Stephens, with the new wave of designers. The Swan 51 was one of the first, a German Frers design developed from the successful *Blizzard*, and *Scoundrel* was launched in 1981 for Bruce Owen, a full-on racing boat with a comfortable interior.

One of the joys of being a Swan owner, or of being associated with one as a crew, is that there are some delightful regattas exclusively for this make of yacht. They are held in the nicest places, Porto Cervo, the Caribbean and even Cowes, and they are probably the most successful of all regattas; as if to prove the point, six boats which were entered for the Rolex World Cup in Porto Cervo in 1986 did not actually race — their owners simply wanted tickets to go to the parties which were only available to competitors!

Four years prior to that delicious piece of social climbing, Bruce Owen took *Scoundrel* to Porto Cervo and returned home with the major prize, the Rolex-Swan World Cup.

Windward Passage

There never has been, and probably never will be, an ocean racer which has so endeared herself to the hearts of the men who go to sea as the 73-footer that Alan Gurney designed, *Windward Passage*.

Windward Passage was built on a beach in Grand Bahama from that loveliest of boatbuilding materials — wood. Her builder was Charlie Tuttle and, sixteen years after he had completed her, Charlie was married aboard his creation in Sydney Harbour. The crew, who attended, were in their uniforms, which led navigator Peter Bowker to remark that it was the first time he had been to a wedding in shorts!

Windward Passage was designed when the maxi limit was 73 ft overall and rigged as a ketch — spar technology in those days was not up to single-masted maxis — and from the outset was always in the hunt for line honours. None of her three owners has ever let her age stand in the way of progress and she has been constantly updated, achieving a new lease of life when she became a sloop. From then on she was able to mix in with the other maxis, using her age allowance and IOR Mark IIIA to keep her within the 70-ft IOR limit. Her undistorted hull shape is not kindly regarded by that rule; justifiably though, *Windward Passage* is a fast boat on any point of sailing.

But surely no boat has been more loved. One February she was in St. Petersburg Yacht Club marina waiting to be sold. She looked dishevelled until one afternoon when a number of sailors who had raced aboard her in the past climbed on with mops and hoses and gave her a thorough clean. They could not bear to see her looking anything less than perfect.

Name of yacht:– WINDWARD PASSAGE	
Registered:	United States of America 1978
Designer:	A.Gurney
Builder:	C.Tuttle
Materials:	Wood
Length o/a:	22.25 metres (73ft)
Length w/l:	19.81 metres (65ft)
Beam:	5.89 metres (19ft 4in)
Draft:	3.05 metres (10ft)
Displacement:	36,287 kilos (79,940 lb)
Sail area:	232.26 sq.metres (2,500 sq.feet)

Sleeper

Name of yacht:–	SLEEPER
Registered:	United States of America 1985
Owner:	L. North
Skipper:	L. North
Designer:	Nelson/Marek
Builder:	J. Betts Enterprises
Materials:	S-Glass/E-Glass
Launched:	1984
Length o/a:	12.71 metres (41ft 8in)
Length w/l:	10.21 metres (33ft 6in)
Beam:	4.04 metres (13ft 3in)
Draft:	2.28 metres (7ft 6in)
Displacement:	7,525 kilos (16,578 lb)
Rating:	32.8 feet IOR
Sails by:	North
Sail area:	94.70 sq.metres (1,019 sq.feet)

When an internationally renowned sailmaker sells his business, most of the yachting trade takes notice. When he then decides to build and race his own boat rather than someone else's for the first time in many years, almost everyone looks to see what he has chosen. They certainly did when Lowell North commissioned *Sleeper*.

Since he lives in San Diego, it did not take too long to walk around to 2820 Canon Street to discuss his project at the offices of Nelson/Marek, whose growing portfolio included many recent winners. Like many IOR boat-owners, Lowell North had the Admiral's Cup in mind, and the criteria for the United States team selection included a top limit of 33.5 ft rating; he settled for a 42-footer that rated at 32.8 ft IOR.

Fractionally rigged on a displacement of 17,000 lb, she had powerful stern sections which gave her a sparkling performance while reaching and put her at the front of the SORC fleet in 1985 and again in 1986. She went to Newport, Rhode Island, and was selected for the team to go to England.

There, however, life was not all good for the boat with the blue-grey hull. In the first inshore race *Sleeper* ran aground, and then lost what few points she gained following a protest. In the third of the inshore races, in Christchurch Bay — when the American team appeared to come into its own — *Sleeper* was fourth, tied with Denmark's *Euro*, while her team-mates *High Roler* and *Sidewinder* were third and sixth respectively.

UBS Switzerland

For his third entry into the Whitbread Round the World Race Pierre Fehlmann decided that a maxi-rater would have the highest possible profile and the greatest attraction to sponsors. He understood that the public at large only understand the line honours winners and he was determined to have a boat which would reward his sponsors with the greatest amount of publicity.

His approach was first to Bruce Farr, who had designed his previous entry, and then to Decision SA in Geneva to build the craft in the lightest yet strongest possible manner. Fehlmann and Farr ran twelve variations of Farr's design over a computer-simulated course using Fehlmann's wind strengths and point-of-sail forecasts. One of those twelve became *UBS Switzerland* and was to beat the rest by eight hours around the world.

The hull was built of a Kevlar laminate over a Nomex core with an aluminium alloy frame inside to take the stress loadings of the keel and rig. She displaced 63,000lb and, incorporating a keel with a laminar flow bulb, had less wetted surface than any of the other maxis in the race but the longest waterline. She was transported to the water, at Monaco, from Geneva in the hold of a Super Guppy aircraft.

Fehlmann had finished fourth in each of his two previous Whitbreads, but *UBS Switzerland* did almost everything that he could have wanted. He started by being first home to Cape Town and then was third into Auckland, but less than two hours behind the leader. He was first on the third leg and then destroyed the opposition on the final leg, leading into Portsmouth by 40 hours for an elapsed time win 4 days 16 hours better than *Lion New Zealand* and breaking *Flyer's* record by 2 days 16 hours. Fehlmann's cup was full, but on handicap he was, once again, fourth!

Name of yacht:–	UBS SWITZERLAND
Registered:	Switzerland 1985
Owner:	Michel Burckhardt
Skipper:	P. Fehlmann
Designer:	B.Farr
Builder:	Decision SA
Materials:	Kevlar/Nomex/Epoxy
Launched:	1985
Length o/a:	24.50 metres
Length w/l:	19.50 metres
Beam:	5.45 metres
Draft:	4.08 metres
Displacement:	28,544 kilos
Rating:	69.4 feet IOR
Sails by:	Hood
Sail area:	269 sq.metres

Sumurun and Velsheda

Two elderly ladies, as much ocean thoroughbreds as their far younger sisters, *Sumurun* and *Velsheda* have been lovingly restored and given a new lease of life. Both were seen racing in Cowes Week of 1986 and indeed had a match out to the Nab and back which was won by *Sumurun*, the 94-ft ketch designed and built in 1914 by Fife of Scotland for Lord Sackville.

Originally *Sumurun* was rigged as a gaff yawl and described as a fast cruiser, one of the ultimate of her type. She was raced often, particularly against her near sister, *Rendezvous*, and in the big fleet with *Britannia* and *Westward*. Seventy years after her launch she won the Atlantic Cup in the Classic Yacht Regatta at Newport, Rhode Island.

Sumurun's hull and decks are of teak over sawn oak frames and beams, the type of construction guaranteed to last a lifetime, or two. Her deck structures and trim are varnished teak while down below the joinery is of Japanese oak. Now she has all the modern comforts — deep-freezers, a desalination plant and the latest in today's electronics — and is available to a few lucky people for charter after her no-expense-spared restoration.

Velsheda, built by Camper & Nicholson for William Stephenson in 1933, was not much more than a rotting steel hull when she was purchased in 1979 by Terry Brabant. He had ideas — which he openly admitted as being way beyond his station — of restoring the J-class boat to her former glory, or as near to it as he possibly could.

From where *Velsheda* sat, on a slipway on the Itchen opposite the yard where she had been built, Brabant engaged contract craftsmen to help him with what seemed like an impossible task. Ninety per cent of the steel plating was renewed and a hollow steel keel was built under the hull to be filled with lead ingots and, slowly, topped up with molten lead. That exercise saved the costly casting of a new keel — the original one had gone for scrap when the hull was used as a houseboat.

Slowly the whole project came together so that, exactly fifty years to the date of her original launch, *Velsheda* (from the first letters of the names of Stephenson's daughters, Velma, Sheila and Daphne) went down the ways again. Still there is no auxiliary power and *Velsheda* is sailed everywhere, with only the occasional assistance to her berth by a motorboat. She too is available for charter, and a sail on board her is an unforgettable experience.

Name of yacht:—	SUMURUN
Registered:	United States of America 1986
Owner:	A.Towbin
Skipper:	J.Mills
Designer:	W.Fife
Builder:	W.Fife
Materials:	Teak on Oak
Launched:	1914
Length o/a:	28.96 metres (95ft)
Length w/l:	20.73 metres (68ft)
Beam:	5.03 metres (16ft 6in)
Draft:	3.96 metres (13ft)
Displacement:	79,251 kilos (174,590 lb)
Sails by:	A.Cario
Sail area:	325.15 sq.metres (3,500 sq.feet)

Name of yacht:—	VELSHEDA
Registered:	United Kingdom 1985
Owner:	T.Brabant
Designer:	C.Nicholson
Builder:	Camper & Nicholson
Materials:	Steel
Launched:	1933
Length o/a:	38.83 metres
Length w/l:	25.30 metres
Beam:	6.40 metres
Draft:	4.57 metres
Displacement:	145,294 kilos
Rating:	J-Class
Sails by:	Ratsey & Lapthorn
Sail area:	700.65 sq.metres

Victory '83

Victory '83 was the second 12-Metre to be built to Ian Howlett's designs and was commissioned by Peter de Savary for his Royal Burnham Yacht Club challenge for the America's Cup. She was constructed, at Hamble, by Fairey-Allday.

For much of her time in Newport there were experiments with winglets on her keel — not huge lead ones, which did so much to improve the stability and speed of *Australia II*, but wooden ones, weighted to produce passive buoyancy, which were bolted on overnight behind a screen and, more often than not, removed the following evening. It was, however, a confidential request to the IYRU by Howlett for clearance on these winglets that was revealed by de Savary and helped Alan Bond in his fight (with the New York Yacht Club) over the legality of *Australia II*'s winged keel.

Victory '83 faced *Australia II* in the final for the right to challenge for the America's Cup and, with Lawrie Smith as skipper, won the first race but lost the next four in a row. Soon afterwards she was sold to the Consorzio Italia as a base for its first challenge for the Cup.

The following year, *Victory '83* competed in the World Championship at Porto Cervo and beat *Azzurra* in the match race final. She then became the Italian crew's training boat but competed in the World Championship again in 1986 off Fremantle, where she was dismasted. Since this 12-Metre was designed and built in Britain, she could not be considered as a challenge for the Cup in 1987, and was replaced by *Italia*.

Name of yacht:—	VICTORY '83
Registered:	Italy 1986
Owner:	Consorzio Italia
Designer:	Ian Howlett
Builder:	Fairey-Allday
Materials:	Aluminium
Launched:	1983
Length o/a:	19.81 metres
Length w/l:	13.72 metres
Beam:	3.76 metres
Draft:	2.67 metres
Displacement:	25,401 kilos
Rating:	12 Metre class
Sail area:	200 sq.metres

Whirlwind VIII

Name of yacht:–	WHIRLWIND VIII
Registered:	United Kingdom 1981
Owner:	N. Lister
Skipper:	N. Lister
Designer:	Sparkman & Stevens
Builder:	Nautor
Materials:	GRP
Launched:	1981
Length o/a:	23.30 metres
Length w/l:	18.96 metres
Beam:	5.73 metres
Draft:	2.27 metres
Displacement:	48,418 kilos
Rating:	56 feet IOR
Sails by:	Hood
Sail area:	250.5 sq.metres

One can hardly say that any yacht of 76 ft overall is a series production boat; every owner of a boat this size will have a host of different requirements, and Nautor were more than prepared to pander to these whims when they produced this Swan series, of which *Whirlwind VIII* was one of the five built.

Noel Lister commissioned this boat for his charter company, which in turn leased it on many occasions to the members of the management of MFI for a series of 'Outward Bound' style courses in the Mediterranean around Greece and Turkey. Lister's professional skipper, Bill Porter (known as Lord of the Horn for being the only man to have raced three times round Cape Horn within four years), used to conduct these exercises with the military precision of a retired Chief Petty Officer RN. Orienteering, mountaineering and scuba diving all found their way into the courses, while his wife Maggie provided the welcoming food to complement the luxury of the boat. Everyone who took part in them rated the courses highly successful, but then who would not in such surroundings?

Whirlwind VIII was the seventh Swan for Lister, and he extended her cruising from the Mediterranean to the other side of the Atlantic, where she was seen on the eastern seaboard of the United States and in the Caribbean, where she took part in Antigua Race Week. The hull design of the Swan 76 was taken from the highly successful *Kialoa III*, a boat which, when she was retired from racing, was converted by her owner, Jim Kilroy, into a cruising boat similar to a Swan. *Kiaola III* had originally a ketch rig similar to that of *Whirlwind VIII*, one with great ease of handling, but Kilroy decided to stay with the sloop rig which he had ordered for her later racing career when he converted her for cruising.

War Baby
and Volador

War Baby was one of the last of the large, classic, custom-built cruiser/racers to emerge from the design offices of Sparkman & Stephens, and she continued to be a high-profile racer for many years before embarking on some of the most adventurous cruising undertaken by a yacht. She has in her later years been from the Arctic ice to the same limits in Antarctica.

This 62-footer was built, as *Dora IV*, in aluminium alloy by Palmer Johnson in 1972. She was chartered by Ted Turner in the mid-1970s for the SORC, and Turner liked the boat so much that he purchased her and continued to race her under the name *Tenacious*. In 1979, in the storm-tossed Fastnet, *Tenacious* carried all before her, finishing almost three-and-a-half hours ahead of the second-placed boat on corrected time.

The Fastnet win meant much to Turner and his crew, but for one in particular it had a special significance. Peter Bowker had won the Sydney to Hobart Race as Turner's navigator on *American Eagle* in 1972, and eighteen months later did the same job for Chuck Kirsch's *Scaramouche* to win the Bermuda Race; the Fastnet win gave him a unique treble of the classics and was rewarded six months later in Florida when the two skippers awarded him the Golden Dividers Trophy.

War Baby was still racing, at Antigua Race Week in 1986, when she was captured by Beken with *Volador*, an 81-ft ketch designed by German Frers and built in aluminium alloy by Wolter Huisman for Horst Homberg. *Volador's* interior, which includes every conceivable luxury, was designed by Peter Beeldsnigder and is finished in teak and leather.

Her German owner took this magnificent boat to Australia with him, but sold her when he found insufficient time to enjoy her to the full. It is an action he regrets, but one from which Texan Charles Butt has benefited to the full, cruising her in the Caribbean Islands and on the eastern seaboard of the United States.

Name of yacht:–	WAR BABY
Registered:	Bermuda 1983
Owner:	W. Brown
Skipper:	W. Brown
Designer:	Sparkman & Stephens
Builder:	Palmer Johnson
Materials:	Aluminium
Launched:	1972
Length o/a:	18.74 metres (61ft 6in)
Length w/l:	14.02 metres (46ft)
Beam:	4.82 metres (15ft 10in)
Draft:	2.74 metres (9ft)
Displacement:	14,612 kilos
Rating:	45.6 feet IOR
Sails by:	Hood
Sail area:	144 sq.metres

Name of yacht:–	VOLADOR
Registered:	United States 1986
Owner:	C. Butt
Designer:	G. Frers
Builder:	Huisman
Materials:	Aluminium
Launched:	1982
Length o/a:	24.31 metres (79ft 9in)
Length w/l:	19.48 metres (63ft 11in)
Beam:	5.84 metres (19ft 2in)
Draft:	3.0 metres (9ft 10in)
Displacement:	37,511 kilos (82,637 lb)
Sails by:	Hood
Sail area:	221.7 sq. metres (2,386 sq.feet)

Yellowdrama IV

It is one of the apocryphal stories of the marine trade that Ken Cassir only bought this Swan 57 in order to stop John Irving bashing his ear over the telephone and telling him how much he needed one. True or not, Cassir did not regret his purchase, one of the fifty built to this Sparkman & Stephens design since 1977.

Yellowdrama IV has competed in the 'fun' regattas of the world. Here she is enjoying the delights of Antigua Race Week, that annual end-of-the-season (for chartering, at least) regatta where sunshine and regular breeze combine to give all the competitors something to do between the round of beach parties, where the real competitive spirit comes into its own. It is being able to appreciate the correct blend of rum and sun-oil that distinguishes the serious Antigua Race competitor from the common herd, and the crew of *Yellowdrama IV* were among the front-runners.

They were also at the front at the first Swan World Cup at Porto Cervo in 1980 when she was awarded the Concours d'Elegance — not the sort of award which either Peder Lunde or Otto Zehender-Muller were seeking when they entered the Whitbread Round the World Race with their Swan 57s, *Berge Viking* (8th in the 1981-82 race) and *Shadow of Switzerland* (11th in the 1985-86 race).

When *Yellowdrama IV* was sold, Cassir expressed his confidence in the boat by returning to Nautor for her replacement. *Yellowdrama V* was a Swan 651.

Name of yacht:–	YELLOWDRAMA IV
Registered:	United Kingdom 1981
Owner:	K. Cassir
Designer:	Sparkman & Stephens
Builder:	Nautor
Materials:	GRP
Launched:	1980
Length o/a:	17.5 metres
Length w/l:	13.95 metres
Beam:	4.74 metres
Draft:	2.75 metres
Displacement:	19,084 kilos
Rating:	42.8 feet IOR
Sail area:	168.76 sq.metres

Yeoman XXVI

Name of yacht:–	YEOMAN XXVI
Registered:	United Kingdom 1986
Owner:	O. Aisher
Designer:	G. Frers
Builder:	Vision Yachts
Materials:	Nomex/Kevlar/Carbon
Launched:	1985
Length o/a:	13.53 metres
Length w/l:	11.02 metres
Beam:	4.15 metres
Draft:	2.9 metres
Displacement:	8,278 kilos
Rating:	35.2 feet IOR
Sails by:	North
Sail area:	88.45 sq.metres

The latest of a line of racing yachts to bear the famous name of *Yeoman*, number XXVI is the most modern boat for the grand old man of yachting, Sir Owen Aisher. A 44-ft German Frers design, she was built by Vision Yachts at Cowes using Kevlar and carbon fibre over a Nomex core, and was campaigned in the 1985 Admiral's Cup trials.

Subsequently *Yeoman XXVI* completed two further seasons of racing, often skippered by Peter Scholfield, including the 1987 Admiral's Cup trials in which she occasionally made her presence felt to the embarrassment of her younger competitors. At the end of that season she was put in the hands of the brokers to make way for *Yeoman XXVIII* (the intervening number being taken by Sir Owen's son Robin), a boat which was aimed for the 'younger members of the Aisher family'.

The *Yeoman* line began with a ketch in 1936 (winner of the Crankshaw Bowl in the 1947 Round the Island Race) and a 6-Metre, *Yeoman II*, two years later. *Yeoman III* was perhaps the most famous of Sir Owen's yachts. With her he won the Fastnet in 1951 and in two seasons she claimed 52 prizes out of 61 starts; subsequently she became the RORC's club yacht, *Griffin II*. *Yeomans IV – X* and *XII* and *XIV* were all 5.5-Metres, the last of which was sailed by Robin to a bronze medal at the 1968 Olympic Games in Mexico.

It wasn't until 1975 (and again in 1977) that a *Yeoman* was to be selected for an Admiral's Cup team, although *Griffin II* was in the first two series. *Yeoman XX*, the famous Kiss Kiss, produced some awe-inspiring performances to be in the winning team on both occasions.

Yeoman XXIII also made a winning team in 1981.

That *Yeoman*s are always painted green, or at least with a green trim, is due to the Irish heritage of Lady Aisher, who has broken the champagne bottle on the bows of most of them at their launches.

Unbearable, Local Hero IV and Fair Lady

There can be very little better racing than that of the One-Tonners in a fresh breeze. During the Cowes Week of 1986 these three had some superb tussles with the fortunes favouring each of them in turn, yet all three are very different boats, and two of them are off production lines.

Local Hero IV is the one-off. A Philippe Briand design for Geoff Howison, she was modified during the winter of 1985−86 after a moderate first season. She was raced as far afield as the Clyde, for the McEwan Scottish Series, and in the Solent.

Fair Lady was chartered for the season by Ernest Juer, who said that it was like getting back into a dinghy again. She was built by Bénéteau and had been first raced by Eric Duchemin in the 1984 One Ton Cup before being withdrawn, by Brian Sweby, from the following year's Admiral's Cup trials. Juer proved that the boat was still fast by winning the Britannia and New York Yacht Club Cups, a double which few have ever managed but which Juer has now performed twice.

Unbearable began life as *Framboise*, an X One-Tonner designed by Nils Jepperson and built in Denmark. She was purchased at the beginning of 1986 by Kit Hobday, who largely raced her on the East Coast and renamed her to carry his 'Bear' lineage. On a day in Cowes Week he had one race which was quite unbearable.

There are those days when you perhaps wish that you had not bothered to get up. For Hobday this was one of them. His yacht was nicely placed but closing with the shore as she ran back past the Green. A gybe was necessary, and that should not have provided his crew with much of a problem, even if the boat was fractionally rigged and the runner had to come on sharply. But it didn't and a squall hit the boat just as the gybe was made — the result was all too plain to see. *Unbearable*'s racing was over for the day, and there was a fair amount of work to do before she raced again.

Name of yacht:−	UNBEARABLE
Registered:	United Kingdom 1986
Owner:	C. Hobday
Skipper:	C. Hobday
Designer:	N. Jeppersen
Builder:	X-Yachts
Materials:	R-Glass/Kevlar/Carbon/Foam
Launched:	1985
Length o/a:	12.06 metres
Length w/l:	10.13 metres
Beam:	3.72 metres
Draft:	2.22 metres
Displacement:	5,597 kilos
Rating:	30.6 feet IOR
Sails by:	Banks/Mead
Sail area:	80.50 sq.metres